THE
SPIRALIZER
RECIPE BOOK

From Apple Coleslaw to Zucchini Pad Thai,
150 Healthy and Delicious Recipes

CARINA WOLFF

Avon, Massachusetts

Published by
Adams Media, a division of F+W Media, Inc.
57 Littlefield Street, Avon, MA 02322. U.S.A.
www.adamsmedia.com

ISBN 10: 1-4405-9438-4
ISBN 13: 978-1-4405-9438-0
eISBN 10: 1-4405-9441-4
eISBN 13: 978-1-4405-9441-0

Printed in the United States of America.

10   9   8   7   6   5   4   3   2   1

Library of Congress Cataloging-in-Publication Data
Wolff, Carina, author.
The spiralizer recipe book: from apple coleslaw to zucchini pad thai, 150 healthy
  and delicious recipes / Carina Wolff.
Avon, Massachusetts: Adams Media, [2016]
Includes index.
LCCN 2015050524 | ISBN 9781440594380 (pb) | ISBN
  1440594384 (pb) | ISBN 9781440594410 (ebook) | ISBN 1440594414 (ebook)
LCSH: Cooking (Vegetables) | Pasta salads. | Carving (Meat, etc.) |
  LCGFT: Cookbooks.
LCC TX801.W654 2016 | DDC 641.6/5--dc23
LC record available at *http://lccn.loc.gov/2015050524*

Always follow safety and commonsense cooking protocol while using kitchen utensils, operating ovens and stoves, and handling uncooked food. If children are assisting in the preparation of any recipe, they should always be supervised by an adult.

Many of the designations used by manufacturers and sellers to distinguish their products are claimed as trademarks. Where those designations appear in this book and F+W Media, Inc. was aware of a trademark claim, the designations have been printed with initial capital letters.

Cover design by Sylvia McArdle.
Cover and interior photography by Carina Wolff.

This book is available at quantity discounts for bulk purchases.
For information, please call 1-800-289-0963.

DEDICATION

I dedicate this book to my family and friends who have not only consistently encouraged me to turn my love for cooking and writing into a career, but who went out and bought spiralizers of their own after hearing me rave about them incessantly. I want to also especially thank my mom and grandmother, who raised me to pay attention to healthy foods and nutrition at a time when the information wasn't readily available, and my dad for helping me get through the hard parts of chasing my dream by giving me sound support and advice.

Contents

INTRODUCTION

Although we know it's a part of a healthy diet, most of us don't get overly excited about eating our fruits and vegetables. I don't know about you, but when it comes down to having a vegetable-filled salad or a soothing plate of pasta for dinner, I'm going to head straight for those delicious noodles.

But what if I told you there's a way to enjoy the satisfying taste of pasta while still reaping the nutritional benefits of fresh vegetables? With a spiralizer, you're able to have both the veggies and the pasta. In fact, your vegetables become your pasta! It might be hard to imagine a zucchini turning into a beautiful bowl of fettuccine, but with the right tools, you can make a delicious and filling classic noodle dish using just your favorite vegetables. I expect you'll be just as amazed at how satisfying these faux dishes can be as I was when I first discovered the technique. Watching these plain vegetables being transformed into long and spindly noodles, I was instantly hooked.

Using a simple device, spiralizing fruits and vegetables allows you to replace foods like pasta with nutrient-filled produce such as zucchini, sweet potato, and squash. This is a great way for you to cut down on refined carbohydrates and load up on the types of whole foods that are especially healthy for you. Whether you're gluten-free, paleo, or vegan—or have no dietary restrictions at all—using vegetables instead of grains is a great way to switch up your meals and have a little fun in the kitchen,

all while getting healthier in the process. No matter what your culinary needs are, there's always something amazing you can make with a spiralizer.

Though I've mostly mentioned pasta, using a spiralizer goes beyond making just noodle dishes. You can also create other fun recipes such as toppings for salads, fancy desserts, and even perfectly shaped curly fries.

When I first started using the spiralizer, I stuck to simple pasta dishes, oftentimes topping zoodles (zucchini noodles) with marinara sauce or pesto. While that's a convenient and simple use of the device, I eventually came to realize the wonders of this contraption and soon discovered a myriad of crazy meals I could create: a pizza crust made out of potato, rice made from plantains, shoestring fries made from jicama. Experimenting with different blades as well as different types of produce can open the door to so many versatile and healthy meals. The spiralizer transcends all dietary restrictions and the world's cuisines—there's always a dish for everyone, no matter their personal taste or preference.

In this cookbook, you'll find recipes for any type of dish, whether you're attempting a twist on a classic Italian spaghetti, cooking for your gluten-free friends, or making a dessert that's healthy for your kids. Spiralizing will transform the way you cook, and you'll never want to look back at traditional recipes ever again!

CHAPTER ONE

The Basics of Spiralizing Vegetables

The first step in your journey is to pick out a spiralizer. It's important you have a device that fits your needs and the type of cooking you will be doing. Some spiralizers are only able to do smaller, softer vegetables, while others have many different blades and can handle many varieties. Other spiralizers take up much more counter space and are harder to clean, while others fit in a drawer and can be thrown in your dishwasher.

Types of Spiralizers

There are a few different types of spiralizers available on the market, and all of them are relatively inexpensive.

Handheld Spiralizers

Handheld spiralizers tend to be the cheapest and most compact. They slightly resemble large pencil sharpeners, and they are most commonly used with smaller and thinner vegetables such as zucchini. People tend to have trouble using handheld devices with larger, firmer vegetables such as carrots or sweet potatoes. Other larger root vegetables such as beets or parsnips have proven to be nearly impossible to spiralize with these types of devices. Although most handheld spiralizers come with only one blade, some options do come with multiple blades.

Popular and well-reviewed handheld spiralizers include the GEFU Spirelli Spiral Slicer, the Kitchen Supreme Spiral Slicer Spiralizer, and the Spiralizer 4-Blade Vegetable Spiral Slicer.

Vertical-Hold Spiralizers

In these spiralizers, the vegetable sits on top of the blade, making it easier for you to put pressure down onto the vegetable as you spiralize because of the assistance of gravity. Although you get less vegetable waste, it doesn't work with all vegetables, especially larger ones such as butternut squash. Some people tend to have problems with smaller vegetables such as carrots as well because they're too thin to reach the blade.

Vertical-hold spiralizers tend to be more expensive than the handheld versions. Popular brands include the Benriner Cook Helper Slicer and Müeller Spiral-Ultra 4-Blade Spiralizer.

Horizontal-Hold Spiralizers

These type of spiralizers are generally the most popular, as they can spiralize the widest variety of fruits and vegetables. Spiralizers that work horizontally can hold vegetables with greater diameters, so they work great for choices such as beets and squash. Because these spiralizers have three, sometimes four, interchangeable blades, you can also experiment with different shapes, sizes, and textures. This is the type of spiralizer I recommend, as they're the most versatile. They also are reasonably priced.

Well-known horizontal-hold spiralizers include the Brieftons 5-Blade Spiralizer and the Paderno World Cuisine Tri-Blade Plastic Spiral Vegetable Slicer. The Paderno spiralizer is the one I use. They also have a newer, four-blade version, but I, along with many other bloggers and chefs, prefer to use the original three-blade version, as it seems to handle the vegetables better.

Options If You Don't Have a Spiralizer

If you don't own a spiralizer, there are a variety of other kitchen utensils you can use to make noodle dishes. If you don't happen to own any type of special gadgets, you can always get back to the basics and use a knife, cutting vegetables into long strands or thin slices. Below are a few options if you don't have a spiralizer available.

Mandoline

A mandoline slicer doesn't quite produce those long twirly noodles, but it can cut vegetables into long, thin, straight slices that are the next best thing. You just slide your fruit or vegetable across the surface blade, and it produces strands quicker than if you were to use a knife.

Julienne

Julienning is a style of cutting foods into long, thin strips with even sides. You can do it with a knife, but you can also buy julienne peelers that will help get the job done. Julienne slices are usually a bit thicker than mandoline slices, and this can be a good option for wider-noodle dishes.

Peeler

Using a regular old peeler can give you slices that can function as thin, ribbon-like noodles. These noodles will be wider and more delicate than the spiralized version, but they're a good replacement for fettuccine or other wide spiralized options.

Using Different Blades

I use three types of blades for my recipes, and they all come from the Paderno Tri-Blade Spiralizer, although I reference them by generic names so you can use the closest spiralizing method of your choice. They are the following:

Small-Noodle Blade

This blade produces noodles that have the shape and size of spaghetti. It is typically a blade with small, triangular blades (3 mm). This is the most common type of spiralizing blade, and it can be used with almost any type of fruit and vegetable.

Large-Noodle Blade

This blade looks exactly like the small-noodle blade, only its triangle blades are larger (6 mm), producing a wider, thicker noodle. This blade tends to produce noodles with more curl, making it a great option for creating curly fries.

Straight-Noodle Blade

Unlike the first two blades, a straight-noodle blade produces noodles that are wide and ribbon-like. It also functions well as a slicer, making thin cuts in foods like apples and potatoes. It's a good option for chips.

CHAPTER TWO
Fruits and Vegetables Ideal for Spiralizing

Although zucchini and sweet potatoes are probably the most commonly spiralized vegetables, there is a wide array of other fruits and vegetables that can be prepared in the same way. Changing what fruits and vegetables you use will not only keep your meals new and exciting, but it will provide you with a healthy balance of nutrients to make sure you are getting all the vitamins and minerals you need in your diet.

As a rule of thumb, you want to make sure you are choosing fruits and vegetables that are in season and that have been organically grown. Look for produce that is ripe and firm, and be sure to pick a type that is big enough to spiralize. If a fruit or vegetable is too mushy, it won't be able to spiralize, and if it's too small, the noodles will fall apart.

Following are some of the most commonly spiralized fruits and vegetables, with a little bit of information on how to choose them, how they are best prepared, and their most important nutrients.

Apples

Most apples are easy to spiralize, and you don't need to pick out specific ones to obtain good results. Look for apples that are even in shape and size and have no bumps or bruises.

To spiralize apples, just remove the stem. You can use any of the blades for spiralizing apples, but using a straight-noodle blade will have the apples come out as thin slices rather than noodles. You can eat spiralized apples raw, sauté them in a pan, or bake them in the oven. They can be prepared with the peel on or peel off, though the peel provides you with the most fiber. Spiralized apples are best served raw in salads, or served warm with breakfast or desserts.

Apples are high in fiber, low in calories, and contain antioxidants such as polyphenols and vitamin C, which can help boost cardiovascular health and help fight against cancer.

Beets

When purchasing beets, make sure to buy them raw. The larger they are, the easier they are to spiralize. Both red and golden beets work equally well.

Beets need to be peeled before spiralizing, and they can be eaten raw or roasted in the oven. They go well with salads and in Mediterranean or Middle Eastern dishes. Golden beets are a bit more mild than red beets, making them a good pasta substitute (and less messy to prepare).

High in vitamin C, folate, manganese, and fiber, among other nutrients, beets are great cancer fighters and work to detoxify our bodies and fight inflammation.

Broccoli

Broccoli noodles require spiralizing the bottom stalk of the broccoli plant. Be sure to buy the broccoli whole, and choose a stalk that's at least 1½″ wide.

A small-noodle blade is best for spiralizing broccoli, and it can be served raw, sautéed, or roasted. Broccoli noodles are light and mild in flavor, and they taste best with salads or pastas that are lightly dressed.

The stalk of broccoli is higher in fiber than its florets. It also contains some protein, calcium, and iron, and combined with the florets, is high in antioxidants.

Butternut Squash

Choose a squash that is evenly shaped, meaning the bottom part isn't much more bulbous than the top. You will use the top of the squash to spiralize, as the bottom part contains the seeds and cannot be put through a spiralizer.

Butternut squashes are spiralized after the entire outer skin has been peeled and the bulbous bottom portion sliced off entirely. You can use any blade for squash, and it has a taste and texture very similar to spaghetti, making it a great substitute for many types of pasta dishes, though it tends to be a bit on the sweet side.

Extremely high in vitamin A and other antioxidants, butternut squash also contains fiber, vitamin C, vitamin B_6, manganese, and copper. It is also one of the highest plant sources of omega-3 fatty acids.

Cabbage

Green and purple cabbage heads are best for spiralizing, and all you have to do is chop off the bottom and remove the outer layer of leaves.

Although cabbage can be spiralized, it does not come out like noodles and instead comes out shaved or shredded, making it a great choice for salad or coleslaws. It can also be sautéed and served warm or boiled in soups.

Purple cabbage is higher in antioxidants, but both varieties contain fiber, folate, vitamin C, vitamin K, potassium, and other nutrients.

Carrots

Whether it's the orange kind, purple, white, or yellow, any carrot can be spiralized, but you'll have the most luck with thicker, jumbo carrots that are at least 1½″ wide. Bigger carrots are often found fresh, with the leaves still attached, at local farmers' markets or stores with fresh produce.

Carrots are best spiralized using a small-noodle blade, and they can be served raw, roasted, sautéed, or boiled. They have a mild taste, so they can be used with many types of dishes, but spiralized carrots taste especially good in salads or Asian-inspired dishes.

Carrots are extremely high in beta carotene, an antioxidant that converts into the most usable form of vitamin A. They are also rich in potassium, fiber, biotin, vitamin K, and vitamin C.

Celeriac

Celeriac is the root of a celery plant, and it has a tough and hairy exterior that needs to be chopped off and peeled before spiralizing. Look for options that are smooth rather than bumpy. Celeriac is best during its peak season of fall and winter.

This root vegetable is best spiralized with a small- or large-noodle blade and can be served raw, boiled, or roasted. Its taste is similar to that of regular celery, but it also resembles a white potato, with just a bit of nuttiness.

Celeriac is low in calories, and contains fiber, potassium, iron, and vitamin C.

Cucumbers

When shopping for cucumbers to spiralize, look for the larger varieties, such as the garden cucumber, that have wider diameters and will come out as noodles instead of breaking off into little half-moons. You also want your cucumber to be firm, or the noodles will come out too watery or mushy.

You can spiralize cucumbers using any blade, forming them into small or large noodles or wavy ribbons. You can keep the skin on or remove it, although the skin contains many important nutrients. Cucumber noodles are best served raw in salads or cold dishes. Always remove excess water by patting noodles dry with paper towels.

Full of cancer-fighting antioxidants, cucumbers are good anti-inflammatories and are great for keeping the body hydrated, as they are made up of mostly water. They also contain vitamin K, vitamin C, magnesium, and potassium.

Daikon Radish

This radish, a staple in Asian cuisine, has a much larger root and is more conducive to spiralizing than smaller radishes. Look for even and smooth daikon radishes. Although you want your radish wide enough to spiralize, don't go too wide, as it may be difficult to use the vegetable on your spiralizer.

Daikon radish can be served raw or cooked, and tastes best with Asian-inspired meals or in soup. It is best spiralized using a small- or large-noodle blade. To prepare, you can choose to roast, sauté, or boil the radish. The noodles come out firm and crunchy and can withstand many types of cooking or added sauces.

This larger variety of radish is fat-free and low in calories, and it is filled with fiber, vitamin C, and copper, making it a great choice for healthy skin.

Jicama

Chose whole jicamas that are medium in size with unblemished skin. They are best when they are round and firm.

You must peel jicama before spiralizing it, and you can use any size blade. Spiralized jicama can be served raw and eaten as a snack or served in a salad. It can also be seasoned and roasted, making the vegetable softer and taking on a bit of a different flavor. Cooked jicama goes well in spicy dishes or Mexican-inspired plates.

Jicama is low in calories and high in fiber, vitamin C, and potassium. It is low on the glycemic index, making it a good choice for those with diabetes. Jicama also contains vitamin B_6 as well as iron.

Onions

You can spiralize any type of onion, from sweet to yellow to red. Just make sure your onion isn't too mushy; the firmer it is, the more it will hold up when spiralized.

Spiralizing an onion won't turn it into noodles, but it can help shred the onion for raw salads or produce curly pieces you can use for onion rings or onion shoestrings. You can use spiralized onions for any dish that typically calls for onions, especially recipes that require longer, thinner slices rather than diced.

Onions not only add flavor to any type of dish, but they are high in many antioxidants, helping to fight against cancer, cardiovascular disease, inflammation, and loss of bone density.

Parsnips

Parsnips have a similar shape to carrots, so look for medium to large parsnips that are smooth and firm. The larger their diameter, the easier they are to spiralize.

To prepare the parsnip, peel it and spiralize it using the small-noodle blade. It can be sautéed or roasted. Parsnip has a taste and texture similar to potatoes, and since its flavor is pretty neutral, it is a great replacement for pasta as well as a substitute for potatoes in dishes such as soup, fritters, or fried pancakes.

Parsnips are high in soluble fiber, folate, potassium, vitamin C, and vitamin E. They are low in calories and help improve cardiovascular health.

Pears

Like apples, most pears can be spiralized. Look for pears that are even in shape and size and have no bumps or bruises.

To spiralize pears, remove the stem. You can choose to keep or remove the peel, although the peel contains half the fruit's fiber as well as an abundance of nutrients. Any blade can be used to spiralize pears, and you can make them into noodles or shave into ribbon slices. Spiralized pears are best served raw, though you can briefly sauté or roast them to serve them warm.

Pears are high in fiber, antioxidants, vitamin C, and vitamin K. They have wonderful anticarcinogenic properties and can help lower your risk of type 2 diabetes.

Plantains

Although overly ripe plantains do taste delicious in many types of dishes, when it comes to spiralizing you want to look for plantains that are still green, as they will be firmer and more likely to form noodles. You also want to look for a plantain that is more straight rather than curvy.

Plantains do spiralize into noodles, but they are best when prepared as a substitute for rice, either by pulsing them in a food processor or mashing them up in a pan. They work best with Caribbean-inspired dishes, but they also work well as a replacement in any rice dish, whether sweet or savory.

Despite looking like bananas, plantains have their own set of nutrients. They are filled with fiber, vitamin A, vitamin C, vitamin B_6, and potassium.

Potatoes

When it comes to potatoes, opt for the larger varieties such as russet or white potatoes, which will yield the most noodles. The smaller varieties work as well, but the noodles may not come out as even or as plentiful. Any color potato will work.

Using a small-noodle blade will produce noodles very similar to pasta, and a large-noodle blade will create thicker strands that work best as curly fries. The peel can be kept on or peeled off, and potatoes can be baked, sautéed, or fried. They can be used as noodle replacements, or prepared crispy as side dishes or toppings for salads.

Potatoes are high in fiber, antioxidants, vitamin B_6, potassium, and copper. They can help lower blood pressure and fight against cardiovascular disease and cancer. Leave the peel on for more nutrients.

Radishes

The bigger the radish, the better. Since radishes are small, you may not be able to spiralize all of them, but if they are at least 1″ wide, they should work.

You can spiralize radishes into small noodles or use a straight blade to shave them. Serve them raw in salads or use them as toppings for dishes such as toast.

Radishes are low in calories, high in fiber, and contain vitamin C, folates, B vitamins, and vitamin K. They are also great cancer fighters.

Sweet Potatoes

Look for the larger sweet potatoes and ones that are symmetrical in shape. The smaller kinds work as well, but the noodles are more likely to break off, and they will yield a lot less noodles than their larger counterparts.

When spiralizing sweet potatoes, you can leave the peel on or take it off, although removing it makes for softer and smoother noodles if you're using it as a pasta replacement. They can be spiralized with any type of blade. Sweet potato noodles, as per their name, tend to be on the sweeter side, but they can be used for savory dishes as well as sweet breakfasts or desserts.

Sweet potatoes are one of the best sources of vitamin A, given that they are high in carotenoids. They are also very high in vitamin C, manganese, copper, the B vitamins, potassium, and fiber.

Turnips

When choosing turnips, look for those that are medium in size with a smooth exterior. Avoid turnips that are soft and shriveled or have any bruises or blemishes.

Turnips have a slightly peppery, bitter flavor, and they are best prepared roasted, sautéed, or boiled using a small-noodle blade. They can be used in soups, as replacement for pasta, or in salads. As noodles, they are very sturdy and can hold up well with heavier sauces.

Low in calories, turnips contain good amounts of fiber, vitamin C, and vitamin B_6. They also contain some protein, calcium, and potassium.

Zucchini

While shopping for zucchini, opt for the larger kind, as they yield the most even and sturdy noodles. Look for straighter zucchini versus those that are oblong or curvy.

Zucchini can be spiralized using any blade, and they can be prepared with the peel on or off. Since zucchini are soft, they can be used raw as a pasta replacement, or they can be made even softer by sautéing. Their taste is extremely mild, making them a great pasta replacement in almost any dish.

However, be careful with water-based sauces, such as tomato sauce, as it may cause the zucchini to become slightly runny and watery. You can combat this by soaking up excess moisture from zucchini with a paper towel before cooking.

This summer squash is a great source of antioxidants, fiber, vitamin C, magnesium, copper, and manganese. It also helps to regulate blood sugar, fight inflammation, and protect against cancer.

CHAPTER THREE
Breakfasts

Kale and Butternut Squash Frittata

Frittatas are not only a quick way to throw together any leftover ingredients and create a flavorful breakfast dish, but they are great for feeding large amounts of people. If you're not serving a large crowd, they make great meals for the rest of the week! The combinations are endless when it comes to ingredients, but using butternut squash adds a little sweetness and fall flavor. Frittatas are best prepared in a cast-iron skillet, as they cook quite evenly this way, but any oven-safe pan can be used as well.

Serves 4–6

- 1 butternut squash
- 2 tablespoons extra-virgin olive oil, divided
- 1 medium onion
- 4 large cloves garlic
- 2 cups chopped kale
- 6 large free-range eggs
- ½ teaspoon paprika
- ½ teaspoon cumin
- ¼ teaspoon oregano
- 10 cherry tomatoes, halved
- ⅓ cup Parmesan cheese

1 Preheat oven to 400°F. Cut the bulbous end off your butternut squash and set aside. You will be using the longer end to spiralize. Peel butternut squash until the top, tough surface is completely removed and then slice in half crosswise. Spiralize the half without seeds using a small-noodle blade.

2 In a small pan, heat 1 tablespoon olive oil on medium heat. Add squash, cover, and cook for about 5–7 minutes until squash is soft.

3 Dice onion and finely chop garlic. In a separate oven-safe, medium-sized pan or cast-iron skillet, heat remaining 1 tablespoon olive oil on medium-low heat. Add onions, garlic, and kale and cook for about 3–5 minutes until onions are translucent and kale is soft. While mixture is cooking, crack eggs in a bowl and whisk until frothy.

4 Once onions, garlic, and kale are ready, keep flame on and add paprika, cumin, and oregano, mixing in until evenly coated. Add squash and tomatoes, spreading evenly, and then pour eggs on top of mixture. Cook for 2–3 minutes until edges of eggs begin to set. Remove from heat and sprinkle on Parmesan cheese.

5 Transfer pan to the oven and cook for about 10 minutes or until eggs are no longer runny. Let cool for 5–10 minutes and then serve warm.

Quick and Easy Jalapeño Hash Browns

Hash browns are a quintessential brunch food, and these hash browns will make your mid-morning meal extra special with their spicy kick of jalapeño. This potato dish is simple to make and only lightly fried, making it less fattening than your traditional hash browns. By baking the potatoes first, you cut down on both oil and fry time, ensuring that you're starting your day on a healthy, yet delicious, note.

Serves 2 or 3

- 1 large russet potato
- ½ small onion
- 1 small jalapeño
- 2–3 tablespoons extra-virgin olive oil
- 1 teaspoon garlic powder
- 1 teaspoon paprika
- Salt
- Pepper

1 Preheat oven to 350°F. Cut potato in half crosswise and slice off both ends. Spiralize using a small-noodle blade. Cover a baking sheet with aluminum foil and spread noodles evenly on top. Bake for about 10 minutes.

2 While potatoes are baking, dice your onions and jalapeño. When potatoes are finished remove from the oven. Heat 2 tablespoons olive oil in a medium-sized, oven-safe pan on medium-high heat. Add onions and jalapeño, stirring them in the pan to coat with olive oil. Cook for about 1–2 minutes and then add potatoes to the pan. Add another table-spoon of oil if necessary. The more oil you add and the higher heat you use, the more crispy your potatoes will be.

3 Toss the potato, onion, and jalapeño mixture in the pan with garlic powder and paprika until potatoes are coated. Cook for a few minutes, stirring occasionally.

4 Crank the heat to high and form your po-tatoes into a hash brown patty shape using the entire pan. Pat the top of the potatoes down with a spatula to flatten and form. Cook for about 1–2 minutes to solidify patty and to crisp the bottom, but be careful not to burn the potatoes by keeping the flame on for too long. Once patty has solidified, remove from heat and top with salt and pepper as desired.

French Toast with Sweet Pears

French toast can be a decadent breakfast, but one that can get unhealthy really quickly, especially if you are someone who generously piles on the sweets. This easy-to-make, healthified version uses whole-grain bread instead of white bread and spiralized pears for a sweet but natural topping. If you don't have pears, apples are a great substitute as well, and they can be prepared in the same way.

Serves 2 or 3

1 medium pear

1½ tablespoons coconut oil, divided

1 teaspoon cinnamon, divided

½ teaspoon vanilla

¼ teaspoon nutmeg

2 large cage-free eggs

½ cup almond milk

½ teaspoon wild raw honey

4 slices whole-grain bread

Optional: powdered sugar and maple syrup

1 Cut off both ends of pear and spiralize using a small-noodle blade. In a small pan, heat ½ tablespoon coconut oil on medium-low heat. Add pears, ½ teaspoon cinnamon, vanilla, and nutmeg and stir until pears are coated. Cook for about 2 minutes or until pears are soft. Set aside.

2 In a large, wide bowl, combine eggs, almond milk, honey, and ½ teaspoon cinnamon. Whisk until mixture is frothy. In a large pan or skillet, heat 1 tablespoon coconut oil on medium heat. Dip bread into egg mixture until fully coated, and then place bread onto the pan or skillet. Cook for 2 minutes on each side or until bread fluffs up and turns golden brown. You may need to add more coconut oil as you go if pan gets too dry.

3 Top bread with pears and serve warm. If you desire, finish toast off with powdered sugar and maple syrup.

Lemony Herb Zucchini Scramble

This fluffy egg scramble gets its flavor from an abundance of herbs, and using fresh herbs helps diminish the need to season the dish with butter or salt. Throw in some lemon, and you have a fresh and airy breakfast that tastes like it's fresh from the garden. This recipe calls for thyme, basil, and rosemary, but you can also use other herbs such as parsley or oregano.

Serves 2

½ medium onion
2 cloves garlic
1 medium zucchini
2 tablespoons extra-virgin olive oil
1 tablespoon chopped fresh thyme
1 sprig fresh rosemary, chopped
8 fresh basil leaves, chopped
4 large eggs
Zest of 1 lemon
Juice of 1 lemon

1 Finely chop onion and garlic. Cut zucchini in half crosswise and slice off each end. Spiralize using a small-noodle blade.

2 Heat olive oil in a medium pan on medium heat. Add onion and garlic and stir to coat. Cook for 1 minute and then add zucchini, thyme, rosemary, and basil. Cook for another 3–5 minutes until zucchini and onions are soft.

3 While the zucchini, onion, and garlic are cooking, crack eggs into a bowl and whisk until fluffy and bubbly. Lower heat to medium-low and add eggs to pan. Let sit for about 1 minute. While eggs are sitting, add lemon zest and lemon juice. Then, with a spatula, scramble eggs by moving them across the pan continuously until eggs are fully cooked and form soft curds. Serve warm.

Sweet Potato and Kale with a Fried Egg and Maple Mustard Drizzle

Get your fill of antioxidants with this sweet and salty dish that combines the savory flavors of kale, onions, and mustard with the sweet touches of sweet potato and maple syrup. The maple mustard drizzle provides some moisture to an otherwise vegetable-heavy hash. Get ready for your taste buds to explode when the yolk of your egg breaks and oozes together to combine with the sweet maple mustard syrup, making for a unique culinary combo.

Serves 2

4 tablespoons Dijon mustard

4 tablespoons pure maple syrup

2 sweet potatoes

3 tablespoons extra-virgin olive oil, divided

1 cup chopped yellow onions

4 cups chopped kale

2 large eggs

Pepper

1 In a small bowl, mix mustard and maple syrup until smooth and creamy. Set aside.

2 Peel your sweet potatoes. Cut in half crosswise and slice off both ends. Spiralize using a small-noodle blade.

3 In a medium pan, heat 2 tablespoons olive oil on medium heat. Add sweet potato, onions, and kale, tossing so olive oil coats everything evenly. Cover and cook for about 5 minutes, stirring halfway through so nothing burns. Cook until sweet potato is soft, kale is wilted, and onions are translucent. Once everything is cooked, remove the mixture from the pan and place on two plates.

4 In a large pan, heat 1 tablespoon olive oil on medium-low heat. Crack the eggs into the pan and cook until the whites are fully cooked but the yolk is still runny. Remove from pan with a spatula and place eggs on top of hash mixture.

5 Using a spoon, scoop maple mustard sauce from bowl and drizzle over eggs and hash combo, covering evenly. Top with black pepper as desired. Serve warm.

Coconut and Almond Milk Quinoa with Warm Cinnamon Apples and Banana

Many people assume quinoa is just used for lunch or dinner, but quinoa can be prepared sweet and gooey, just like oatmeal. Quinoa is a great way to start the day with protein, especially if you want to skip out on eggs or bacon. Add in the fiber from the apples and you have a balanced meal that will keep you energized throughout the day.

Serves 2

- 1 large apple
- 1 teaspoon coconut oil
- ½ cup almond milk
- 2 cups cooked quinoa
- ½ teaspoon cinnamon
- ¼ teaspoon cardamom
- 1 banana
- 2 teaspoons pure maple syrup
- ¼ cup unsweetened shredded coconut

1 Spiralize apple using a large-noodle blade. Heat coconut oil in a small pan on medium heat. Cook for about 3–4 minutes or until apple is soft but not mushy.

2 In a small saucepan, heat almond milk until it almost reaches a boil. Remove from heat and add quinoa, cinnamon, and cardamom and stir together until evenly mixed. Transfer to a bowl.

3 Slice the banana crosswise. Add banana and warm apples to quinoa bowl. Top with maple syrup and shredded coconut. Add more almond milk if desired.

California Eggs Benedict with Potato

Whenever I go to brunch, my go-to order is eggs Benedict. Although it's extremely delicious and filling, it's not the most nutritious option, so if I'm ever craving the dish, I like to make a version of my own. This eggs Benedict is made "California style," which means it's vegetarian, and loaded with spinach, tomatoes, and avocado instead of Canadian ham. The hollandaise sauce is also lightened up, as I use ghee (clarified butter) and mustard in this easy blender version that doesn't require a double boiler.

Serves 1 or 2

3 egg yolks
2 tablespoons lemon juice
½ tablespoon Dijon mustard
1 large russet potato
4 tablespoons extra-virgin olive oil, divided
Salt
Pepper
Garlic powder
2 cups spinach
½ heirloom beefsteak tomato
3 large cage-free eggs
½ avocado, cut into slices
1 tablespoon white wine vinegar
⅓ cup ghee
Thyme, to taste

1 Begin the hollandaise sauce by putting egg yolks, lemon juice, and mustard into a blender cup, without blending yet. You will want to blend everything together right before serving.

2 Peel potato, cut in half crosswise, and slice off both ends. Spiralize using a small-noodle blade. Heat 1 tablespoon olive oil in a large pan on medium heat. Add potato noodles to the pan, adding a dash of salt, pepper, and garlic powder. Cook potatoes for 7–8 minutes.

3 While potatoes are cooking, heat 1 tablespoon olive oil in a separate large pan on medium heat. Add spinach and cook for about 2 minutes or until spinach begins to wilt. Remove from pan and set aside.

4 Cut 2 thin slices from the tomato and add to pan; cook for 1 minute on each side to soften. Set aside with spinach.

5 Once potato is ready, remove from pan and place into a medium bowl. Crack 1 egg into a small bowl and whisk. Mix potato noodles with the egg until evenly coated. Divide noodles into 2 ramekins and press down on the top of the potato to flatten and form a bun shape.

6 Heat 2 tablespoons olive oil on medium heat. Add potato buns from ramekins to pan, keeping their shape, and press flat with a spatula. Cook for about 3–4 minutes on each side until crispy. You may need to add more olive oil to the pan if the buns begin to dry out. Once they are finished, remove from pan. Top with spinach, tomato, and sliced avocado.

7 To poach remaining eggs, fill a deep, wide pan with about 1" of water. Add white wine vinegar and bring to a boil. Crack each egg into a small ramekin. Bring water to boil, and use a spoon to swirl the water in one direction. Carefully transfer each egg from the ramekin into the center of the whirlpool. Cook for 4–5 minutes and remove eggs with a slotted spoon. Place eggs on top of avocado.

8 Prepare hollandaise by heating ghee in a saucepan on medium heat until hot and melted. Add to blender a little at a time, pulsing so sauce becomes frothy. Pour immediately over Benedict, and top with a dash of thyme, to taste.

Tips for Hollandaise Sauce
It's important you prepare the hollandaise sauce right before serving, as its texture will change if it's left sitting. Also, be careful to slowly add the butter to the blender, so as to not burn yours if it's plastic.

Potato Pancakes with Chives

Even if you aren't celebrating the Jewish holiday Hanukkah, there's always time to eat a delicious potato pancake. Usually deep-fried, this version is only lightly fried in olive oil, and it's prepared with parsley and chives, giving the dish a little bit of a punch. You can serve these potato pancakes by themselves, or you can try pairing them with poached or fried eggs or topping them with the traditional sour cream and applesauce combination (though I suggest using Greek yogurt instead of sour cream for a healthier meal).

Serves 3 or 4

2 large russet potatoes

2 large eggs

2 tablespoons chopped fresh parsley

1 tablespoon whole-wheat flour

1 teaspoon garlic powder

4 tablespoons vegetable oil

2 tablespoons chopped chives

Salt

Pepper

1 Cut potatoes in half crosswise and slice off both ends. Spiralize using a small-noodle blade and place into a large bowl.

2 Add eggs, parsley, whole-wheat flour, and garlic powder and stir until potatoes are evenly coated.

3 In a large pan or skillet, heat vegetable oil on medium heat. Use your hands to form little patties with the potato batter and place into the pan. Use a spatula to flatten patties. Cook for about 4 minutes on each side until inside of potatoes look soft and outside is crispy.

4 When potatoes are done cooking, remove from pan and sprinkle with chives and a dash of salt and pepper.

Coconut Cinnamon Sweet Potato Waffles with Blueberries and Maple Syrup

When you think of an indulgent breakfast treat, it's hard not to imagine a plate of warm waffles smothered in sugary treats. If you're trying to eat well, a plate of sugar and refined carbs is not a good way to start the morning. But what if you could substitute white flour with, let's say, a vegetable? You'll be amazed at how easily you can turn a sweet potato into a delicious waffle, and it only requires an egg, plus any flavors you want to add in. Not only is this waffle filled with nutrients and protein, but it will satisfy that sugary breakfast craving without the added sugar.

Makes 4 waffles

2 medium sweet potatoes
2 tablespoons coconut oil
1 large egg
1 teaspoon cinnamon
½ cup shredded coconut
Nonstick cooking spray
1 cup blueberries
2 tablespoons pure maple
  syrup

1   Preheat your waffle iron. Peel the sweet potatoes and spiralize using a small-noodle blade. Heat 2 tablespoons coconut oil in a large pan on medium heat. Add sweet potatoes, cover, and cook for 7–9 minutes or until soft.

2   In a large bowl, combine sweet potatoes with the egg, cinnamon, and shredded coconut. Spray waffle iron with nonstick cooking spray, and pour the sweet potato batter into the waffle iron. You may have to use a spoon to get the potatoes into the divots. Cook for about 5 minutes on medium or according to your waffle settings.

3   Top with blueberries and maple syrup and serve warm.

Savory Waffles
Waffles don't have to stop at sweet potatoes. Try experimenting with other vegetables such as potatoes or parsnips for savory waffles that can be paired with eggs or made into a sandwich.

Avocado Toast with Zucchini Ribbons and Almond Pesto

Avocado toast is having a moment right now, but the simple breakfast dish can get boring pretty fast. Why not spruce up your avocado toast by adding some toppings? Since zucchini is soft, it blends well with the smooth texture of avocado, and a little dash of almond pesto gives your breakfast a zesty punch. You'll also get some morning protein and a boost of brain power from the almonds, which contain vitamins and minerals that can help improve your energy and focus throughout the day.

Serves 4

4 slices whole-grain bread
2 large ripe avocados
1 zucchini
½ tablespoon extra-virgin olive oil

Ingredients for Almond Pesto
2 tablespoons raw almonds
1 cup arugula
1 clove garlic
Juice of 1 lemon
2 tablespoons extra-virgin olive oil
Optional: red chili flakes

1 Lightly toast bread in the toaster oven until golden. While bread is toasting, slice avocados in half and remove the pit. With a fork, scoop out both avocados and place in a small bowl. Mash avocado with fork until mostly smooth, with a few chunks here and there. When bread is done toasting, remove from toaster oven and spread avocado evenly on top of each slice.

2 Cut zucchini in half crosswise and slice off each end. Spiralize using a straight blade so it comes out into ribbons. Heat ½ tablespoon olive oil in a small pan on medium-low heat. Cook for about 2–3 minutes until zucchini has softened up a bit. Remove from pan and spread on top of avocado.

3 To make pesto, add almonds, arugula, garlic, lemon juice, and olive oil to a blender or food processor and blend until smooth. Spoon on top of zucchini, top with red chili flakes if desired, and serve immediately.

Keeping Your Toast Fresh
If you need to let your toasts sit before serving, be sure to squeeze a little bit of lemon juice over the avocado to help prevent it from turning brown. The citric acid helps keep the avocado fresh, and the lemon flavor will only enhance the taste once you serve.

Apple Maple Bacon Oatmeal with Cheddar Cheese

It doesn't matter if you're an oatmeal person or a bacon person, because now you can have both in the morning! This sweet and savory dish combines all the elements of breakfast and will have you wishing it's fall all year round. If you want to make this a vegetarian option, feel free to take out the bacon. Or, if you don't have any bacon on hand, any type of sausage can work as well.

Serves 2

2 cups water

1 cup old-fashioned oats

1 medium apple

½ tablespoon coconut oil

½ teaspoon cinnamon

1 tablespoon olive oil

4 strips uncured, applewood-smoked bacon

1 tablespoon pure maple syrup

2 tablespoons shredded sharp Cheddar cheese

1 Boil water in a small pot. When water begins to bubble, add oats. Stir and reduce to simmer. Cover and cook for about 5 minutes or according to package.

2 While oatmeal is cooking, spiralize apple using a small-noodle blade. Heat coconut oil in a small pan on medium heat. Add apples and cinnamon and toss apples in oil until they are evenly coated. Cook for about 5 minutes or until apples are soft.

3 To prepare bacon, heat olive oil in a pan on medium heat. Add bacon strips and cook for about 2 minutes on each side or until crispy. Remove bacon from pan and cut into small pieces.

4 When oatmeal is done, place into a bowl and top with apples, bacon, maple syrup, and Cheddar cheese, allowing cheese to melt from the heat of the other ingredients. Serve warm.

Golden Beet Egg Bites

These quick-bake, little egg bites are a great option if you're serving multiple guests or want to prepare breakfast that will last you the entire week. They're quick to throw together, and you can customize them or switch them up each week by adding in different spiralized vegetables or other toppings. These egg bites are on the sweeter side, thanks to the golden beets, but you can sprinkle some cheese on them or add some pepper to balance out their flavor.

Makes 12 egg bites

8 small beets

2 tablespoons extra-virgin olive oil, divided

½ medium onion

4 cloves garlic

8 large cage-free eggs

¼ teaspoon salt

½ teaspoon pepper

Nonstick cooking spray

1 Preheat oven to 425°F. Peel beets and slice off both ends. Spiralize using a small-noodle blade. Place noodles evenly on a baking sheet lined with aluminum foil (you may need to use 2 baking sheets). Drizzle with 1 tablespoon olive oil and bake for 10–15 minutes until beets are soft. When beets are done cooking, lower oven temperature to 375°F.

2 Chop onion and garlic. In a medium pan, heat 1 tablespoon olive oil on medium-low heat. Add onion and garlic and cook for about 3–4 minutes or until onion is almost translucent.

3 In a large bowl, beat eggs until they are frothy and bubbly. Add beets, onions, garlic, salt, and pepper and mix together.

4 Spray a muffin tin with nonstick cooking spray and transfer egg mixture into tins. Bake at 375°F for 20 minutes. Let cool for 5–10 minutes and then pop eggs out of muffin tin using a fork. Serve warm.

Poached Eggs over Zucchini Ribbons with Avocado, Asparagus, and Spinach Basil Pesto

This green bowl is bursting with nutrients, including healthy fats from the avocado, protein from the poached eggs, and an abundance of vitamins and minerals from the zucchini and pesto. The zucchini ribbons make a great soft base for the poached eggs, and the asparagus adds a bit of a crunch. If you find that poaching eggs is too complicated, you can substitute them with runny sunny-side-up eggs or soft-boiled eggs instead.

Serves 2

- **4 tablespoons extra-virgin olive oil, divided**
- **9 spears mini asparagus**
- **1 large zucchini**
- **½ cup spinach**
- **½ cup basil**
- **1 tablespoon pine nuts**
- **1 clove garlic**
- **Juice of 1 lemon**
- **1 tablespoon filtered water**
- **½ avocado**
- **1 tablespoon white wine vinegar**
- **2 large cage-free eggs**

Struggling with Your Poached Eggs?

If you enjoy a poached egg but can't seem to get it right, consider buying an egg poacher, which can ensure perfectly shaped eggs if you aren't able to execute it on your own.

1 To cook asparagus, preheat oven to 425°F. Drizzle 1 tablespoon olive oil over asparagus spears and roast for 15–20 minutes.

2 Slice zucchini in half and cut off both ends. Spiralize using a straight-noodle blade, so the noodles come out thick and wavy. Heat 1 tablespoon olive oil in a large pan on medium heat. Add zucchini and cook for 3–4 minutes or until they begin to get soft but not wilted. Place into a bowl.

3 Add spinach, basil, pine nuts, garlic, 2 tablespoons olive oil, lemon juice, and filtered water to a blender and blend together until smooth. Set aside.

4 When asparagus is finished, chop into small pieces. Dice avocado and top zucchini with asparagus and avocado.

5 To poach eggs, fill a deep, wide pan with about 1" of water. Add white wine vinegar and bring to a boil. Crack each egg into a small ramekin. Bring water to just boil and use a spoon to swirl the water in one direction. Carefully transfer each egg from the ramekin into the center of the whirlpool. Cook for 4–5 minutes and remove eggs with a slotted spoon.

6 Transfer eggs to zucchini bowl and drizzle with pesto. Enjoy warm.

Brussels Sprouts and Potato Hash with Eggs

Although they used to be a food many people feared, Brussels sprouts have been making a comeback in the culinary world. Prepared correctly, Brussels sprouts are quite good, especially when their texture is balanced by the softness of something like potatoes and a creamy egg yolk. Be careful not to overcook your Brussels sprouts, as not only do they begin to lose their nutritional value if they're cooked too much, but they also begin to take on a pretty foul taste and smell. The key is to keep them slightly crunchy rather than completely tender.

Serves 2

- 1 medium russet potato
- 4 tablespoons extra-virgin olive oil, divided
- 2 cloves garlic
- ½ medium onion
- 1½ tablespoons chopped shallots
- 3 cups shaved Brussels sprouts
- 2 large cage-free eggs

1 Cut potato in half crosswise and cut off both ends. Spiralize using a small-noodle blade.

2 Heat 1 tablespoon olive oil in a large pan on medium heat. Add the potatoes, cover, and cook for 6–7 minutes, stirring occasionally.

3 While potatoes are cooking, chop garlic and onion. Then in a separate large pan, heat 2 tablespoons olive oil. Add garlic, onions, shallots, and Brussels sprouts; cook for about 5–7 minutes. When mixture is done cooking, transfer to the pan with the potatoes and mix thoroughly.

4 Heat the remaining 1 tablespoon olive oil on medium-low heat. Crack eggs in the pan and cook for about 3 minutes until whites are cooked and egg yolk is runny. When eggs are finished, place on top of potato mixture and serve warm.

Vegetarian Breakfast Burrito Bowls

When I wake up starving and want to have a really hearty breakfast, I always crave a breakfast burrito. Although they are extremely filling and quite tasty, sometimes they're not exactly the healthiest option. These bowls contain all the classic ingredients of a breakfast burrito, but they're served without the tortilla, making them instantly healthier. This recipe doesn't include cheese, so it's good for anyone who is lactose intolerant or doesn't eat dairy. However, if you want a little extra gooeyness and saltiness in your bowl, you can top your bowl with Cheddar cheese or a Mexican blend.

Serves 2

- ½ large onion
- 2 cloves garlic
- 1 large russet potato
- 3 tablespoons extra-virgin olive oil, divided
- 1 teaspoon garlic powder
- 1 teaspoon paprika
- ¼ teaspoon pepper
- 1 cup chopped bell peppers (any color)
- 5 large cage-free eggs
- ½ cup black beans
- ½ avocado, sliced
- 1 tablespoon chopped green onion
- Hot sauce, to taste

1 Chop onion and garlic. Set aside.

2 Cut potato crosswise and slice off both ends. Spiralize using a small-noodle blade. In a bowl, toss noodles with ½ tablespoon olive oil, garlic powder, paprika, and pepper.

3 Heat 1 tablespoon olive oil in a large pan on medium heat. Add potatoes, cover, and cook for about 10 minutes or until potatoes are almost soft.

4 In a separate large pan, heat 1 tablespoon olive oil. Add onions, peppers, and garlic and cook for about 7 minutes or until onions are translucent.

5 While vegetables are cooking, prepare eggs. Crack eggs in a medium bowl and whisk together until frothy. Heat ½ tablespoon olive oil in a small pan on medium-low heat. Add eggs and let sit for about 30 seconds. Once the eggs have cooked a little, drag the spatula across the pan, moving the eggs around to scramble them. Repeat until eggs are fully scrambled, about 3 minutes.

6 Add eggs to 2 bowls and top with onion mixture, potatoes, black beans, avocado, green onions, and hot sauce as desired.

Shakshouka

If you've ever traveled to the Middle East, you may have encountered shakshouka, a dish of eggs simmered in a tomato-based sauce enjoyed by Israelis, Moroccans, and Tunisians alike. There are many variations of the ancient dish, but all you really need is a little bit of tomato sauce and eggs, and you have an instant breakfast. Shakshouka is often supplemented with greens, different spices, or even yogurt, so feel free to get creative—it's hard to make this savory breakfast taste bad.

Serves 3 or 4

1 medium onion

2 tablespoons extra-virgin olive oil

1 cup chopped bell peppers (I used red, green, and yellow)

4 cloves garlic, chopped

1 teaspoon cumin

½ teaspoon paprika

½ teaspoon red chili flakes

Dash of pepper

1 (14.5-ounce) can diced tomatoes

½ cup tomato sauce or marinara

5 large cage-free eggs

Parsley, to garnish

1 Preheat oven to 375°F. Cut off both ends of the onion and remove the outer layer. Spiralize using a small-noodle blade.

2 In a large skillet, heat olive oil on medium heat. Add onions and bell peppers. Cook for about 10 minutes; then add garlic and cook for an additional 2 minutes.

3 Add cumin, paprika, red chili flakes, and pepper and mix in evenly. Add diced tomatoes and tomato sauce or marinara and stir everything together. Cook for about 3–5 minutes until tomato mixture begins to bubble. Crack eggs into skillet, transfer to the oven, and bake for 12–15 minutes or until eggs are set. If you don't want to use the oven, you can also cover the skillet and cook for 5–10 minutes or until eggs cook. Add a few parsley leaves as garnish and serve warm.

Southwest Jicama Breakfast Scramble

The same typical breakfast food can get old, which is why it's nice to sometimes start your morning off with foods you usually associate with lunch or dinner. This fusion breakfast is filled with flavorful spices, eliminating the need for any heavy sauces or cheeses. With the protein-filled combination of black beans and eggs, you'll be sure to stay satiated for a few hours, and the jicama provides you with extra fiber, making this a well-balanced meal to begin your day. If you want to add extra heat, add some cayenne pepper. You can also add some jack cheese if you want a bit of extra flavor.

Serves 3–4

- ½ medium onion
- 1 medium jicama
- 2 tablespoons extra-virgin olive oil
- 1 teaspoon paprika
- 1 teaspoon cumin
- 1 teaspoon oregano
- 1 teaspoon chili powder
- 1 cup corn
- 5 large cage-free eggs
- 1 cup canned black beans, rinsed and drained
- 1 cup quartered cherry tomatoes
- 1 tablespoon chopped cilantro
- 1 medium avocado
- 4 stalks green onion
- Juice of ½ lime
- ¼ teaspoon pepper

1 Dice onion. Peel jicama and cut off both ends. Spiralize using a small-noodle blade, pressing lightly so noodles come out a bit softer. Heat olive oil in a large pan on medium heat. Add onions and cook for 3–4 minutes. Then add jicama noodles along with paprika, cumin, oregano, and chili powder, mixing spices in to jicama. Add corn and cook for 7–8 minutes.

2 While jicama mix is cooking, crack eggs into a bowl and beat until frothy. When jicama is finished, lower heat and add black beans, tomatoes, and cilantro. Then turn heat to medium-low and add the eggs, moving and mixing them around constantly in the pan until cooked, about 2 minutes. Remove from pan.

3 Dice avocado and chop green onion and then sprinkle atop egg mixture. Season with a little bit of lime juice and pepper and serve warm.

CHAPTER FOUR
Salads and Dressings

Vegan Kale Caesar Salad with Roasted Chickpea Croutons

There's nothing like a good Caesar salad, but no one likes to ruin a healthy bowl of greens by pouring on a heavy and fattening dressing. This vegan version of Caesar dressing has been a huge hit with all my vegan and nonvegan friends alike, and since it is made with cashews instead of dairy, you are actually getting an extra boost of protein and fiber. Cashews must be soaked overnight to ensure a smooth and creamy consistency, but it will be worth the wait once you realize how close this dairy-free version is to the real deal.

Serves 2

2 small sweet potatoes

5½ tablespoons extra-virgin olive oil, divided

½ cup canned chickpeas, rinsed and drained

½ teaspoon paprika

½ teaspoon cumin

½ teaspoon garlic powder

½ cup soaked raw cashews

3 tablespoons Dijon mustard

Juice of 1 lemon

1 clove garlic

5 cups kale

8 cherry tomatoes, halved

Cashews Not Blending Smoothly?
If your blender isn't strong enough to get those cashews nice and creamy, try boiling some water first, then soaking the cashews in the warm water. This should help soften them up more so than soaking them in lukewarm water.

1 Preheat oven to 350°F. Peel sweet potatoes, cut in half crosswise, and slice off both ends. Spiralize sweet potatoes using a small-noodle blade. Toss in 1 tablespoon extra-virgin olive oil until evenly coated. Place on a tinfoil-lined baking sheet and cook for about 15–20 minutes or until potatoes are crispy.

2 Increase oven heat to 425°F. Spread aluminum foil over a small baking sheet. Spread chickpeas over foil and drizzle with 1 tablespoon extra-virgin olive oil. Toss with paprika, cumin, and garlic powder until chickpeas are evenly coated. Bake for about 25 minutes or until chickpeas are golden and crispy.

3 While chickpeas are baking, prepare your dressing. Blend cashews, mustard, lemon juice, 2½ tablespoons extra-virgin olive oil, and garlic in a blender or food processor until creamy. If your dressing is too thick, add more olive oil as desired.

4 Put kale into a medium-sized bowl and drizzle remaining 1 tablespoon extra-virgin olive oil over leaves, tossing to coat. Massage kale by rubbing the leaves between your hands, using your fingers to soften the leaves.

5 Toss the massaged kale with the dressing until all leaves are evenly coated. Top salad with tomatoes, sweet potatoes, and crispy chickpeas.

Picnic Potato Noodle Salad

If you're headed to a summer picnic or potluck, you don't want to bring a salad filled with greens that will only wilt by the time you arrive at your gathering. Wow partygoers with this potato salad, a spiralized twist on a classic potato and green bean salad. This recipe is also dairy-free and gluten-free, so none of your allergy-prone friends have to worry about trying your contribution to the potluck.

Serves 2

1 large russet potato
1 tablespoon olive oil
1 cup green beans
⅓ cup chopped sweet onions
8 cherry tomatoes, halved

Ingredients for Lemon Mustard Dressing

1 tablespoon Dijon mustard
Juice of 1 lemon
1 tablespoon extra-virgin olive oil
½ teaspoon dried parsley
Black pepper, to taste

1 Peel potato and cut in half crosswise. Slice off ends. Spiralize using a small-noodle blade.

2 In a medium-sized pan, heat 1 tablespoon olive oil on medium heat. Add potato noodles and cover. Cook for about 8 minutes, stirring occasionally so potatoes don't get mushy or burn. Potatoes should be soft but still hold their shape. Remove from heat and place in a bowl.

3 Add green beans to a medium saucepan and fill it with just enough water to cover green beans. Bring water to a boil and then remove from heat. Let green beans sit for about 5 minutes or until slightly tender. Drain and add to bowl with potato noodles. Add onions and cherry tomatoes.

4 To make dressing, combine mustard, lemon, extra-virgin olive oil, parsley, and black pepper until smooth. Toss dressing with the rest of the salad ingredients until evenly coated. Serve warm or refrigerate.

Mexican Kale Salad with Spicy Avocado Dressing and Shoestring Fries

If you've ever gotten a salad and wished you had a plate of French fries instead, this dish is for you. Taking inspiration from Mexican food, this salad contains fresh ingredients such as onion, tomato, and avocado that work together to create a salad that definitely does not lack flavor. If spiciness isn't your thing, leave out the jalapeños in your dressing, and you're good to go. If you like heat, feel free to add a bit more jalapeño to really pack a punch.

Serves 2–3

- 1 medium russet potato
- 2 tablespoons extra-virgin olive oil, divided
- ½ teaspoon paprika
- 5 cups kale
- ½ teaspoon salt
- 1 cup canned black beans, rinsed and drained
- 4 tablespoons chopped green onion
- 6 cherry tomatoes, halved or quartered

Ingredients for Spicy Avocado Dressing

- 1 large ripe avocado
- ¾ cup cilantro
- 3 tablespoons chopped jalapeño
- Juice of 3 lemons
- 4 tablespoons extra-virgin olive oil
- 1 tablespoon apple cider vinegar

1 Preheat oven to 425°F. Cut potato in half crosswise and cut off both ends. Spiralize using a small-noodle blade, pressing lightly so noodles come out stringier. Spread potato noodles evenly on an aluminum-foil-lined baking sheet so that potatoes aren't covering each other. Drizzle with 1 tablespoon olive oil and sprinkle on paprika. Toss if necessary to coat evenly. Bake for 20–25 minutes or until potatoes are brown and crispy, but check before they're ready so they don't burn.

2 Put kale into a large bowl. Drizzle with 1 tablespoon olive oil and ½ teaspoon salt. Massage kale by rubbing the leaves between your hands, using your fingers to soften the leaves. Add black beans, green onion, and cherry tomatoes.

3 To make dressing, blend avocado, cilantro, jalapeño, lemon juice, olive oil, and apple cider vinegar in a blender or food processor until smooth. Dressing will be thick, but feel free to add more olive oil if you prefer it thinner. Toss dressing with salad ingredients and then top with crispy shoestring potatoes.

Roasted Carrot Quinoa Salad with Baby Kale and White Beans

This rainbow salad is vegan and gluten-free, and you know that it's going to be full of nutrients when there's so much color. I like to prepare a cup of quinoa by cooking it in water at the beginning of the week to use for various salads, and if you have ready-made quinoa or any other grain like brown rice or farro on hand, the preparation time for this salad is extremely quick.

Serves 2

2 large carrots

3 tablespoons extra-virgin olive oil, divided

1 teaspoon cumin

1 teaspoon oregano

1 teaspoon thyme

½ cup cooked quinoa

2 cups baby kale

¼ cup chopped red onion

⅔ cup canned white beans, rinsed and drained

½ cup chopped sun-dried tomatoes

¼ cup chopped fresh parsley

Juice of 2 small lemons

Salt

Pepper

1 Preheat oven to 425°F. Slice off both ends of carrots. Spiralize using a small-noodle blade. Spread noodles evenly on a tin-foil-lined baking sheet and drizzle with 1 tablespoon olive oil. Sprinkle cumin, oregano, and thyme evenly on top of carrots. Bake for about 10 minutes or until carrots are soft.

2 Combine quinoa, kale, onion, white beans, sun-dried tomatoes, and parsley in a bowl. Add carrots and toss with remaining 2 tablespoons olive oil and lemon juice. Add salt and pepper to taste.

Balsamic Spinach Salad with Figs and Avocado

You no longer have to chop onions until there are tears pouring down your cheeks—you can now spiralize them and get them all cut up in a flash! This sweet salad screams summer with its juicy figs, creamy avocado, and refreshing cherry tomatoes, and putting it over a bed of spinach allows the tartness of the balsamic vinegar to come out. If you don't have spinach, this salad can be created with any other green, and you can substitute fruits like strawberries or peaches for the figs.

Serves 2

4 cups spinach leaves

½ medium red onion (¼ cup spiralized)

½ large avocado

10 cherry tomatoes, halved

½ cup canned chickpeas, rinsed and drained

4 figs, halved

Extra-virgin olive oil

Balsamic vinegar

1 Spread spinach evenly on a plate or in a bowl.

2 Cut off the ends of your half onion. Spiralize using the small-noodle blade. Then slice the onion a few times to make strings smaller to evenly distribute throughout salad. Add on top of spinach.

3 Slice avocado into wedges. Add to salad along with tomatoes, chickpeas, and figs. Drizzle olive oil and balsamic vinegar to taste.

Citrus Celeriac Salad with Lemon Cumin Dressing

You may have had a celery salad before, but you most likely haven't had celeriac, also known as celery root. This variety of celery can be spiralized and used as a great neutral base for salads. If the thick noodles are too intense for you, you can make them a little more mild by using the small-noodle blade and breaking the noodles into pieces. This will help the vegetable mix in more with the other ingredients, although the citrus dressing will help add to the celeriac noodles' flavor and distract from its distinct texture.

Serves 2 or 3

1 celeriac root
1 medium grapefruit
1 blood orange
2 tablespoons halved
    hazelnuts
1 tablespoon finely chopped
    fennel bulb

Ingredients for Lemon Cumin Dressing

2 tablespoons extra-virgin
    olive oil
1 tablespoon white wine
    vinegar
1 tablespoon lemon juice
½ teaspoon cumin

1 Cut off outside skin of celeriac root and peel entire outside until smooth. Slice off top and bottom of celeriac and spiralize using a large-noodle blade. Place into a bowl.

2 Cut grapefruit and orange into slices. Use a knife and scoop slices out of peel, removing the whites. Slice grapefruit and orange into cubes. Add to bowl with celeriac, along with hazelnuts and fennel.

3 To make dressing, mix oil, vinegar, lemon juice, and cumin in a bowl until smooth. Drizzle over salad and enjoy immediately or serve chilled.

Prevent Celeriac from Browning
If you want your celeriac salad to have a pretty appearance, prepare celeriac in a timely manner once exposing the vegetable to the air. It can brown quickly, so drop the noodles into a bowl of lemon water if you need to buy yourself some time.

Garlic Lemon Kale Salad with Golden Beets and Chickpeas

Most people enjoy their salads with red beets, but those who may be afraid of the intense flavors of the darker variety may enjoy the mildness of golden beets. They are a great addition to salads, as they're a good source of fiber, helping you stay full, and they're also rich in other nutrients such as potassium and calcium. This salad is simply dressed with garlic paste and lemon, making it a great side dish for many different types of meals. This dish can also easily be made vegan or dairy-free by removing the Parmesan cheese and instead topping the dish with nutritional yeast or even a type of nut.

Serves 2

2 large golden beets

2 tablespoons extra-virgin olive oil, divided

4 cups kale

¼ teaspoon salt

2 cloves garlic

Juice of 2 lemons

½ cup canned chickpeas, rinsed and drained

½ cup cherry tomatoes, chopped

2 tablespoons Parmesan cheese

¼ teaspoon pepper

1 Preheat oven to 425°F. Peel beets and cut off both ends. Spiralize using a small-noodle blade. Place on a baking sheet lined with aluminum foil and drizzle with 1 tablespoon olive oil. Bake for about 15 minutes or until beets are soft.

2 Place kale in a large bowl. Add 1 tablespoon olive oil and salt. Massage kale by rubbing leaves between your hands until they have softened. You want these leaves to be extra soft so they absorb your garlic paste later on.

3 Finely mince your garlic. You want it to form a paste, so if you have chopped it a bunch and it isn't getting any smaller, try adding a little bit of salt into it to soften. Keep mincing until it is very fine and gooey.

4 Add garlic and lemon juice to kale and toss until kale leaves are evenly coated in garlic paste and lemon.

5 Top kale with chickpeas, tomatoes, and finished beets, breaking up the noodles if necessary. Finish off with Parmesan cheese and pepper.

Autumn Harvest Salad

This salad can be made any time of year, but its main ingredients are harvested in the cooler months. In this vegetarian salad, you get a good balance of ingredients, including nuts, seeds, and greens. Dressed in an apple cider vinaigrette, this salad has a slightly sweet taste, which can help balance out the bitterness of the kale.

Serves 2

1 large butternut squash

2 tablespoons extra-virgin olive oil, divided

¼ cup pine nuts

5 cups kale

½ teaspoon sea salt

2 tablespoons pomegranate seeds

Ingredients for Apple Cider Vinaigrette

2 tablespoons apple cider vinegar

2 tablespoons olive oil

½ tablespoon Dijon mustard

½ tablespoon raw wild honey

1 Preheat oven to 400°F. Cut the bulbous end off your butternut squash and set aside. You will only be using the longer end to spiralize. Peel butternut squash until the top, tough surface is completely removed; then slice in half crosswise and cut off the remaining end. Spiralize using a small-noodle blade.

2 Place noodles on an aluminum-foil-lined baking sheet and drizzle with 1 tablespoon olive oil. Bake for 10–12 minutes or until noodles become soft.

3 When squash is ready, remove from the oven. Lower oven temperature to 375°F. Spread pine nuts on a baking sheet and roast for 5 minutes. Remove from oven.

4 Remove stems from kale and place the leaves into a large bowl. Add 1 tablespoon olive oil and salt. Massage kale by rubbing the leaves between your hands, using your fingers to soften the leaves. Add squash, pine nuts, and pomegranate seeds.

5 In a small bowl, mix together apple cider vinegar, olive oil, mustard, and honey. Pour over salad and toss until dressing evenly coats the salad and the ingredients are mixed thoroughly.

Swirly Cucumber Greek Salad

If you've ever been to Greece, then you know how fresh, light, and more importantly, simple their traditional Greek salad is. There's no lettuce and no fancy or heavy dressings—just the classic combination of cucumber, tomato, and onions topped with feta cheese, oregano, and olive oil. This spiralized twist on the famous Greek salad uses thick cucumber noodles, but it keeps the same elements that make their popular salad so great. If you want this salad to turn into a complete meal, try adding some grilled chicken or white fish for a balanced lunch or dinner.

Serves 2 or 3

1 large English cucumber

14 cherry tomatoes

½ medium onion (white or red)

2 tablespoons extra-virgin olive oil

1 tablespoon white wine vinegar

2 ounces feta cheese

Juice of 1 lemon

1 teaspoon oregano

Black pepper, to taste

1 Cut your cucumber in half and slice off the ends. Using the straight blade, spiralize your cucumber and place in between two paper towels, soaking up the excess moisture. Place into a large bowl.

2 Chop cherry tomatoes into halves or fourths, depending on how big the tomato is. Finely dice onion. Add to bowl with cucumber along with olive oil and vinegar. Toss until mixture is evenly coated. Top with feta cheese, either by slicing into cubes or crumbling with your fingers.

3 Finish off salad with lemon juice, oregano, and black pepper. Serve immediately.

Blotting Cucumber Noodles
Whenever you spiralize cucumber, it's important to press the noodles between two paper towels to take out moisture. Otherwise, when combined with sauce or dressing, they'll become too fragile and watery.

Beet Salad with Lentils and Goat Cheese

This salad is made with raw beets, which makes your preparation time quick, especially if you have already-cooked lentils on hand. While the beets, goat cheese, and lentils work together to create a Middle Eastern flavor, you can also substitute chickpeas for lentils, which will give your salad a Mediterranean flair. You can also spruce up the salad by adding walnuts or onions, which gives it a little extra crunch.

Serves 4

- ½ cup uncooked lentils (or 1 cup cooked lentils)
- 2½ cups water
- 6 cups arugula
- 4 large red beets
- 2 tablespoons crumbled goat cheese
- 2 tablespoons extra-virgin olive oil
- 1 tablespoon balsamic vinegar

1 In a medium pot, bring lentils and water to a boil. Once water has started boiling, reduce heat to a simmer and cook for about 30–40 minutes or until lentils are almost soft. Remove from heat and set aside; let cool for 10–15 minutes.

2 Add arugula to a large bowl. Peel beets and slice off both ends. Spiralize using a small-noodle blade. Add to bowl with arugula.

3 Add lentils, goat cheese, extra-virgin olive oil, and vinegar to the bowl and lightly toss. Serve immediately.

Spicy Pickled Cucumber Salad

If you like pickles, you'll love this pickled cucumber salad—their lighter, less sour cousin. You can leave the salad to marinate for only an hour if you're in a rush, but if you have the time, you can allow the salad to sit in the fridge and really soak in the flavors. Just be sure to thoroughly pat your cucumber dry before marinating it, or you'll end up with a puddle of liquid at the bottom of your bowl. If you don't like heat, you can leave out the red chili flakes for a more mild and sweet version.

Serves 2–3

1 large cucumber
¼ small onion, thinly sliced
¼ cup white wine vinegar
1 teaspoon sugar
1 clove garlic, minced
1 teaspoon red chili flakes

1 Cut off both ends of cucumber and spiralize using a straight blade. Place cucumbers between two paper towels and press down, soaking up any extra moisture. Remove from towels and place cucumber in a large bowl. Add onions and toss.

2 In a small saucepan, add vinegar, sugar, garlic, and red chili flakes. Bring to a boil and then remove from heat. Pour mixture over cucumbers and onions and toss until everything is coated. Let marinate in the fridge for at least 1 hour. The longer you let the cucumbers sit, the stronger their pickled flavor will be. Serve chilled.

"Creamy" Spiralized Broccoli Israeli Couscous Salad

Most of us tend to only eat broccoli florets, never even giving second thought to eating the stalk of a full head of broccoli. Turns out, this stalk actually tastes good, and it can be easily spiralized! Now when you buy broccoli, you no longer have to feel guilty about wasting any parts of the vegetable. This salad is vegetarian, but if you want to make it vegan, just leave out the Parmesan and Greek yogurt. The dressing won't be creamy, but it will still be strong enough to flavor the salad.

Serves 2–4

1½ cups whole-wheat Israeli couscous

2 full heads broccoli, stalk included

4 tablespoons pine nuts

1 cup cherry tomatoes, halved

1 cup canned chickpeas, rinsed and drained

½ cup shaved Parmesan cheese

Ingredients for Creamy Lemon Dressing

¼ cup Greek yogurt

1 tablespoon extra-virgin olive oil

Juice of 1 lemon

½ tablespoon white wine vinegar

1 tablespoon Dijon mustard

1 Prepare couscous first according to package (1 cup uncooked yields about 2 cups). Let couscous cool and then add to a large bowl. Chop off broccoli stalks from head. Slice a little bit off both ends so they're flat. Spiralize using a small-noodle blade. Then take the florets from one head of broccoli and chop them up. Add noodles and broccoli florets to couscous. Add pine nuts, tomatoes, chickpeas, and Parmesan cheese.

2 In a small bowl, combine Greek yogurt, olive oil, lemon juice, vinegar, and mustard until smooth. Pour on top of salad and toss until salad is coated evenly. Serve immediately or refrigerate.

Beet and Quinoa Salad with Mint Yogurt Dressing

Roasted beets really pack a punch with their flavor, so much so that they can almost carry their own when it comes to salad. In this salad, however, the flavor doesn't stop there. The richness of the root vegetable is enhanced by the fresh and creamy elements of the Mint Yogurt Dressing, which adds a tang to an otherwise smooth salad.

Serves 2

3 large red beets
1 tablespoon extra-virgin
   olive oil
Dash of salt and pepper
2 cups cooked quinoa
1 cup arugula
¼ chopped onion

Ingredients for Mint Yogurt Dressing
½ cup Greek yogurt
¼ cup fresh mint leaves
1 clove garlic
A little less than ¼ cup white
   wine vinegar
½ tablespoon olive oil
Juice of 1 small lemon
1 teaspoon wild raw honey

1 Preheat oven to 425°F. Peel beets and cut off both ends. Spiralize using a small-noodle blade. Place on an aluminum-foil-lined baking sheet, spreading beets evenly. Drizzle extra-virgin olive oil evenly over beets and season with a dash of salt and pepper. Bake for 15 minutes or until beets are soft.

2 While beets are cooking, add quinoa, arugula, and onions to a large bowl; mix together. Prepare dressing: Add Greek yogurt, mint, garlic, white wine vinegar, olive oil, lemon juice, and honey to a blender or food processor and blend until smooth.

3 When beets are finished roasting, slice them a few times with a knife to break up the noodles. Add to quinoa mixture and add the dressing. Toss until dressing evenly coats all salad ingredients. Serve chilled.

Chopped Pear and Gorgonzola Salad with Kale and Walnuts

Pear and gorgonzola are a classic combination. Throw in some kale, and you have a sophisticated salad that is not only bursting with flavor but boasts a plethora of healthy nutrients. The walnuts give this otherwise soft salad a light crunch and added dose of protein, but you can also top this salad with additions such as chickpeas or chicken if you want to take this dish from a side salad to a full meal.

Serves 4

1 pear
5 cups chopped kale
3 tablespoons extra-virgin olive oil, divided
½ teaspoon salt
⅓ cup Gorgonzola cheese
½ cup chopped walnuts
¼ cup chopped red onions
1 tablespoon balsamic vinegar

1 Cut off both ends of pear and spiralize using a small-noodle blade. Go over the pear noodles with a knife a few times to break up large noodles so they can be tossed in the salad. Set aside.

2 In a large bowl, combine kale, 1 tablespoon olive oil, and salt. Massage kale by rubbing the leaves between your hands, using your fingers to soften the leaves.

3 Add pears, gorgonzola, walnuts, and onions. Toss with 2 tablespoons olive oil and balsamic vinegar. Serve immediately or refrigerate.

Belgian Endive Salad with Apple and Goat Cheese Lentils

If you're sick of the typical green lettuce salad, Belgian endive is great to use because it can be served whole and filled with food, or you can slice it up for a refreshing crunch. This recipe uses a spiralized apple, lentils, and goat cheese filling for a salad that can work well as an appetizer or a light main dish. When choosing your lettuce, be sure to choose Belgian endive, as regular endive such as escarole or frisée won't work for this type of salad.

Serves 4

1 head Belgian endive

1 apple

1 cup cooked black lentils

2 tablespoons crumbled goat cheese

Ingredients for Shallot Dressing

1 tablespoon minced shallots

1 tablespoon Dijon mustard

2 tablespoons extra-virgin olive oil

3 tablespoons white wine vinegar

1   Trim ends of endive and remove leaves from stem to create little boats. Lay them flat across a plate.

2   Spiralize apple using a small-noodle blade. Using a knife, break the noodles into smaller pieces and place into a bowl. Toss together with lentils. Spoon apple-lentil mixture evenly atop each of the endive leaves. Sprinkle with goat cheese.

3   To make dressing, combine shallots, mustard, olive oil, and vinegar in a blender or food processor and blend until smooth. Drizzle over endive and lentil mixture and serve.

Chinese Chicken Salad

A popular restaurant favorite is the Chinese chicken salad, which is actually more of an American dish than a Chinese one. This light and healthy version uses three types of spiralized vegetables: green cabbage, red cabbage, and carrots, making it a quick meal to prepare. This salad is brimming with protein, from the chicken breasts to the edamame to the peanuts. If you want to make the salad more citrusy, you can also add mandarin oranges, which give a little softness to an otherwise crunchy salad.

Serves 4

2 free-range boneless, skinless chicken breasts

1 medium head green cabbage (2 cups spiralized)

1 medium head red cabbage (2 cups spiralized)

2 medium carrots (1 cup spiralized)

¼ cup chopped green onion

½ cup organic edamame

½ cup peanuts

Ingredients for Soy Ginger Dressing

1½ tablespoons soy sauce

½ tablespoon rice vinegar

2 tablespoons sesame oil

½ tablespoon white wine vinegar

1 teaspoon shredded ginger

1 clove garlic, minced

1 Preheat oven to 350°F. Place chicken breasts on a baking sheet and bake for 30 minutes.

2 While chicken is baking, spiralize both types of cabbage using the straight-noodle blade. Cabbage will come out shredded. Place 2 cups of each cabbage into a large bowl.

3 Spiralize carrots using a small-noodle blade. Add 1 cup spiralized carrots to the bowl with cabbage, along with green onion, edamame, and peanuts.

4 When chicken is ready, shred it using your fingers. Add to the bowl and toss ingredients together.

5 To make dressing, mix soy sauce, rice vinegar, sesame oil, white wine vinegar, ginger, and garlic together. Pour into salad bowl and toss until evenly coated. Serve immediately or chilled.

Summery Lemon Dill Zucchini Salad

Since zucchini is so soft it doesn't always have to be cooked to be enjoyed as noodles, which makes it a great option for salads. This light and refreshing zucchini salad includes the addition of asparagus, giving it a little more texture and flavor. It's drizzled with a light Lemon Dill Dressing, making it a great appetizer or even a main meal, since it's so high in fiber. Throw in some chickpeas or white beans for extra nutrients if desired, or enjoy this simple, bright salad as is.

Serves 2–4

- 1 bunch asparagus
- 1–2 tablespoons extra-virgin olive oil
- 3 medium zucchini
- ½ medium red onion
- 1 cup cherry tomatoes
- ¼ cup shredded Parmesan cheese

Ingredients for Lemon Dill Dressing

- 1 tablespoon fresh chopped dill
- Juice of 2 lemons
- 1 tablespoon extra-virgin olive oil
- Salt
- Pepper

1 Preheat oven to 400°F. Cut off the end stalks of the asparagus. Spread asparagus on an aluminum-foil-lined baking sheet and drizzle with 1–2 tablespoons olive oil. Bake for 20 minutes.

2 Cut zucchini in half and slice off both ends. Spiralize using a small-noodle blade. Place into a large bowl.

3 Remove outer skin from onion and slice off both ends. Spiralize using a small-noodle blade. Add to bowl with zucchini.

4 Chop cherry tomatoes and asparagus and add to bowl. Add Parmesan cheese as well.

5 In a small bowl, add dill, lemon juice, olive oil, and a dash of salt and pepper. Add to salad bowl and toss.

CHAPTER FIVE
Soups and Sandwiches

Kale and White Bean Soup with Sweet Potato

This vegan soup is your answer to a quick and low-maintenance meal on a busy night. It only takes about 30 minutes to prepare the soup, and when you're finished, you have enough for a full, balanced meal for four or a side dish or appetizer for larger groups. This soup is served with French bread for garnish, but that is optional, as the soup is hearty and filling on its own. The white beans are a good source of vegetarian protein, and the kale and sweet potato contain not only fiber but calcium, vitamin C, and other important nutrients.

Serves 4–6

2 medium or large sweet
   potatoes
2 tablespoons extra-virgin
   olive oil, divided
1 cup chopped onions
4 cloves garlic, chopped
6 cups kale
4 cups vegetable broth
2 (15-ounce) cans cannellini
   beans, rinsed and drained
1 teaspoon fresh thyme
½ teaspoon pepper

1 Preheat oven to 425°F. Peel sweet potatoes and then spiralize using a small-noodle blade, pressing lightly so the noodles come out stringier. Place on a baking sheet lined with aluminum foil and drizzle with 1 tablespoon olive oil. Bake for 10–15 minutes until noodles are soft and almost crisp.

2 In a large pot, heat 1 tablespoon olive oil on medium heat. Add onions and garlic and cook for about 3–4 minutes until onions are translucent but not yet starting to brown.

3 While onions are cooking, chop kale leaves to fit into the pot; they don't have to be finely chopped. Add vegetable broth to the pot with onions, followed by the kale and white beans.

4 Add thyme and pepper and stir ingredients together. Bring to a boil, then reduce to a simmer and cook for 15–20 minutes. Serve with slices of French bread and top with more pepper as desired.

Grilled Cheese with Squash and Sage

Taking classic comfort foods and making them a little bit more gourmet and a little bit more nutritious is one of my favorite things to do in the kitchen. While a traditional grilled cheese tastes good on its own, there's so much you can do with different combinations of cheese, herbs, and vegetables, and why not stick some veggies in there to add more nutrients into your meal? This recipe calls for Cheddar cheese, but you can get creative and blend cheeses, or opt for another variety such as goat cheese or fontina.

Serves 1

1 medium butternut squash
  (1 cup spiralized)
2 tablespoons extra-virgin
  olive oil, divided
5 fresh sage leaves
2 slices whole-grain bread
½ cup shredded Cheddar
  cheese

1   Cut off bulbous part of squash and set aside. Slice off other side of remaining squash in half crosswise and peel until tough layer of skin is removed. Spiralize squash using a small-noodle blade.

2   In a small pan, heat 1 tablespoon olive oil on medium heat. Add squash and sage, cover, and cook for about 5–7 minutes until squash is soft.

3   Place 1 slice of bread on the counter. Add cheese and squash to that side and then press down and cover with the other slice. Heat 1 tablespoon olive oil in the pan on medium heat. Add to pan, swirling oil around so it coats the bread. Then press down on the bread with a spatula and cover. Cook for about 1 minute and then flip the bread. Cook for another 1–2 minutes or until bread is brown and crisp and cheese is gooey.

Vegetarian Pho with Daikon Radish Noodles

Pho (pronounced "fuh") is a traditional Vietnamese street-food noodle soup that has grown in popularity in the United States in recent years, and for good reason. It's filled with herbs and spices, and comes in many different variations. This vegetarian pho is made at its simplest and can be spruced up to your liking. If you want to add meat to this soup, just prepare it beforehand and drop it into the broth. You can also add ½ tablespoon fish sauce for extra flavor.

Serves 2

- 1 large daikon radish
- 4 cloves garlic
- 1 tablespoon extra-virgin olive oil
- 4½ cups vegetable broth
- 2" piece ginger
- 1 stick cinnamon
- 1 star anise
- 2 cloves
- Juice of ½ lime
- ¼ cup chopped cilantro
- ½ jalapeño, thinly sliced
- ½ cup mung bean sprouts
- 2 stalks green onion, chopped

1. Peel the daikon radish. Cut in half crosswise and slice off both ends. Spiralize using a small-noodle blade. Set aside.

2. Finely chop garlic. In a large saucepan, heat 1 tablespoon olive oil on medium heat. Add garlic, stir, and cook for 2 minutes. Then add broth, whole ginger, cinnamon stick, star anise, and cloves. (This is where you can add fish sauce if you choose to use it, though this will mean the broth is no longer vegetarian). Bring to a boil. Reduce to a simmer, add radish noodles, and cook for 20 minutes.

3. When broth is done cooking, add lime juice, and remove whole ginger, cinnamon stick, star anise, and cloves before serving. Separate soup and noodles into two bowls and top with cilantro, jalapeño, bean sprouts, and green onion. Serve warm.

Vegetarian Zucchini-Noodle Ramen

Ramen has gone from a high-sodium, poor man's dinner to a gourmet and highly revered trendy food enjoyed by people of many cultures. It's a go-to comfort food on chilly days, which makes sense because it's not only filled with strong and savory flavors, but it contains so many ingredients in just one bowl. This version of ramen is vegetarian friendly, as it's made with vegetable broth, and it uses peeled zucchini in place of ramen, which surprisingly does a great job of mimicking ramen noodle's texture. To get a stronger-flavored broth, simmer for at least an hour, but if you're trying to prepare your soup in a hurry, just 30 minutes will do.

Serves 2

- 1 large cage-free egg
- 4 cloves garlic
- 1½ tablespoons fresh minced ginger
- 1 tablespoon sesame oil
- 4 cups vegetable broth
- 2 tablespoons soy sauce
- ¾ ounce dried shiitake mushrooms
- 2 medium zucchini
- 1 stalk green onion
- ½ sheet nori (seaweed)
- Optional: red chili flakes

1 Add egg to a small saucepan and fill with water. Bring water to a boil and then turn off heat. Let egg sit for 6 minutes, then drain water and cool egg with cold water to stop it from cooking. Set aside.

2 Finely mince garlic. Heat 1 tablespoon sesame oil in a medium saucepan on medium-low heat. Add garlic and ginger and cook for about 2 minutes. Then add vegetable broth, soy sauce, and dried mushrooms and bring to a boil. Once broth is boiling, reduce to a simmer, cover, and cook for 30–60 minutes.

3 While broth is cooking, prepare zucchini ramen noodles. Peel your zucchini, cut in half crosswise, and slice off both ends. Spiralize using a small-noodle blade.

4 Finely chop green onion and slice seaweed sheet lengthwise. Peel shell off boiled egg and cut in half. When broth is finished cooking, add zucchini noodles. Serve topped with green onion, seaweed, and boiled egg. Top with red chili flakes for spiciness if desired.

Avocado Sprouts Sandwich with Spiralized Cucumber and Pesto

Sometimes your body just needs a break from meat. When I feel this way, especially if I've fallen off the wagon and eaten something junky, I crave fresh vegetables and light and airy sandwiches or salads. Eating foods like that can be really refreshing, but not always filling. You won't have that problem with this sandwich. Loaded with healthy fats from the avocado, fiber from the spiralized cucumber, and protein from the nuts in pesto, you have a filling but plant-based meal that will have you craving vegetables all day every day.

Serves 1 or 2

2 slices whole-grain bread

1 medium or large ripe avocado

½ cucumber

2 slices from a large tomato

½ cup clover or alfalfa sprouts

2 tablespoons Almond Pesto (see Avocado Toast in Chapter 3)

1 Lay 1 slice of bread flat on the counter. Slice the avocado in half, scoop out both sides with a fork, and place onto bread. Mash avocado down with a fork until mostly smooth, leaving a few chunks here and there.

2 Cut off both ends of your halved cucumber and spiralize using a straight blade so the noodles come out like ribbons. Place in between two paper towels and pat down to soak up excess moisture. Place on top of avocado. Top with sliced tomato and sprouts.

3 On the other slice of bread, spread pesto evenly. Cover other half with this slice of bread. Press the pieces of bread together so sandwich stays firm.

Vegan Tofu Banh Mi Sandwich

Banh mi are traditional Vietnamese sandwiches that come from the French influence in Indochina. They are typically served with pork belly as well as garnishes such as carrots, daikon radish, cilantro, chilies, and cucumber. This sandwich contains all the classic ingredients but replaces pork belly with lemongrass-marinated tofu. You really get to put your spiralizer to work for this sandwich, which contains spiralized cucumber, carrot, and daikon radish. Just give yourself an hour to marinate your tofu as well as your carrots and daikon radish before you plan to eat your sandwich for maximum flavor.

Serves 2

8 ounces extra-firm tofu

2 tablespoons soy sauce

1 tablespoon sesame oil

1 tablespoon lemon juice

3 tablespoons minced lemongrass

1 jumbo carrot or 2 smaller carrots (1 cup spiralized)

⅓ daikon radish (1 cup spiralized)

½ cup white wine vinegar

½ tablespoon sugar

2 tablespoons vegenaise

2 (6") French rolls

1 tablespoon coconut oil

1 medium cucumber (½ cup spiralized)

1 tablespoon cilantro

Got Some Time?
If you're not in a rush, or if you are able to prepare ahead, marinate the tofu and pickled carrots and radish for longer than 1 hour. This will really enhance their flavor and give your sandwich a bit more pizazz.

1 Slice tofu into ½" slices and place in a medium bowl. In a separate small bowl, combine soy sauce, sesame oil, lemon juice, and lemongrass and mix together. Pour over tofu slices and cover. Refrigerate for at least 1 hour.

2 Spiralize carrots and daikon radish using a small-noodle blade (peel radish and then slice off both ends of carrot and radish to spiralize). Place into a small bowl. Combine vinegar and sugar and pour over carrots and radish. Cover and refrigerate for at least 1 hour.

3 Spread 1 tablespoon vegenaise on each French roll. When tofu is done marinating, heat coconut oil in a medium pan. Add tofu and cook for about 3 minutes on each side until golden.

4 While tofu is cooking, spiralize cucumber using a large, straight noodle blade so it comes out in ribbons. When tofu is finished cooking, add tofu to French roll. Top with cucumber, carrots, radish, and cilantro. Serve immediately.

Smørrebrød, Two Ways

Hailing from Denmark, smørrebrød are open-faced sandwiches, typically on rye bread, that consist of different toppings and spreads, from veggies to meat to cheese. There are many combinations you can use for smørrebrød, especially with your spiralizer. Here I've created a chicken apple salad as well as a vegan option made with horseradish cashew cream. Both are tasty and pair well together, but you can also eat them alone, as they are both filling and abundant in protein.

Each recipe serves 2

Ingredients for Chicken Apple Smørrebrød

1 free-range boneless, skinless chicken breast

2 slices rye bread

½ apple (about 1 cup spiralized)

¼ cup Greek yogurt

1 tablespoon Dijon mustard

1 tablespoon apple cider vinegar

1 tablespoon finely chopped parsley

Ingredients for Vegan Horseradish Cream with Radish Smørrebrød

2 slices rye bread

¾ cup raw cashews

1 teaspoon horseradish

¼ cup filtered water

1 teaspoon garlic powder

2 red radishes

½ tablespoon finely chopped fresh chives

For Chicken Apple Smørrebrød

1   Preheat oven to 350°F. Place chicken breast on a baking sheet and bake for 30 minutes.

2   While chicken is baking, toast slices of rye bread. When chicken is finished, let cool. Shred with your fingers or with a fork. Add to a medium bowl.

3   Spiralize apple using a small-noodle blade. Using a knife, break noodles into smaller pieces. Add to the bowl with chicken, along with Greek yogurt, Dijon mustard, and apple cider vinegar. Mix together until ingredients are well combined. Spread on each slice of rye bread and top with finely chopped parsley.

For Radish Smørrebrød

1   Toast slices of rye bread. Add cashews, horseradish, water, and garlic powder to a blender or food processor and blend until smooth. It may take a few minutes for all the cashews to blend evenly.

2   Slice off both ends of radishes and spiralize using a straight-noodle blade. Using a knife, spread cashew cream evenly over rye bread. Top with spiralized radish and finely chopped chives.

Potato and Mushroom Stew with Cabbage

Cabbage isn't the most glamorous of foods, but it can really add some heartiness to something like a soup. Not only that, but it's in the same family as kale and broccoli, making it a good source of vitamins and nutrients along with antioxidants. This stew gets its added flavor from the potato noodles and mushrooms, along with a touch of parsley and basil.

Serves 6

- ½ large onion
- 4 cloves garlic
- 3 tablespoons extra-virgin olive oil
- 1 large russet potato
- ½ medium head cabbage
- 2 cups chopped mushrooms
- 4 cups vegetable broth
- ¼ cup chopped parsley
- ½ teaspoon basil
- ¼ teaspoon pepper

1 Chop onions and garlic. Heat 3 tablespoons olive oil in a large pot on medium heat. Add garlic and onions and cook for 4 minutes.

2 While onions and garlic are cooking, cut potato in half crosswise and slice off both ends. Spiralize using a small-noodle blade. Add potatoes to pot and cook for another 4 minutes.

3 Remove outer layer of cabbage and slice off the bottom end. Spiralize using a straight-noodle blade, so the cabbage comes out in shreds. Add cabbage to pot, along with mushrooms, vegetable broth, parsley, basil, and pepper.

4 Bring broth to a boil and then reduce to a simmer and cover. Cook for about 30 minutes and then serve warm.

Vegan Veggie Burger with Turnip

Veggie burgers are great alternatives to meat patties, but oftentimes store-bought varieties don't contain protein or are filled with processed ingredients and additives. Making your own veggie burger at home is not that difficult or time-consuming, and you can fill it with completely whole ingredients. This burger is filled with lentils, beets, and mushrooms, and is topped with chard, smashed avocado, and crunchy turnip noodles, but just like any burger, you can add whatever condiments you desire.

Serves 4–6

- 2 cloves garlic
- 1 tablespoon extra-virgin olive oil
- ½ cup chopped onions
- ½ cup chopped white mushrooms
- 1½ cups cooked lentils
- ½ cup shredded beets
- 1 teaspoon salt
- ½ teaspoon pepper
- ¼ teaspoon nutmeg
- ½ teaspoon cumin
- 1 teaspoon paprika
- ½ cup walnut meal
- 2 medium avocados
- 4–6 whole-wheat hamburger buns
- 6 teaspoons mustard
- 3 rainbow chard greens
- 1 large tomato
- 1 medium turnip

1 Preheat oven to 375°F. Chop garlic. In a large pan, heat olive oil on medium heat. Add onions, garlic, and mushrooms and cook for 4–5 minutes until onions and mushrooms are soft.

2 Add lentils, beets, salt, pepper, nutmeg, cumin, and paprika. Remove from heat and add walnut meal (to make walnut meal, put walnuts into a food processor or blender and blend until powdery). Mix together until even.

3 Cover a baking sheet with aluminum foil. Form lentil mixture into patties using your hands and add to baking sheet (should make 4 large patties or 6 smaller ones). Bake for 40–45 minutes or until patties are firm.

4 Slice avocados in half. Scoop out avocado and place into a bowl. Mash with a fork.

5 Separate hamburger buns. Spread mustard on the bottom half and smashed avocado on the top. Split chard leaves in half and add one to the bottom of each bun. Slice tomato into ½″ slices and place on top of chard leaves. Top with a burger patty.

6 Peel turnip and cut off both ends. Spiralize using a small-noodle blade. Break noodles with a knife and place on top of each patty. Add burger bun top and serve warm.

Baked Falafel with Spiralized Cucumber

Although falafel hails from the Middle East, you would be hard-pressed to find someone who hasn't enjoyed, or at least heard of, the chickpea sandwich. They are now found all over the world, from street vendors to fancy restaurants and even health-food restaurants. The key to making a healthy falafel is baking it, not frying it, but sometimes getting the perfect consistency can get tricky. These falafel sandwiches are not only vegan, but they are gluten-free as well, as this recipe only uses almond flour to help bind the patties together.

Makes 6 falafel (3 sandwiches)

Ingredients for Falafel

1 (15-ounce) can chickpeas, rinsed and drained
1 tablespoon chopped walnuts
2 cloves garlic
¼ cup chopped parsley
¼ cup chopped cilantro
2 tablespoons lemon juice
3 tablespoons extra-virgin olive oil, divided
1 teaspoon cumin
½ teaspoon coriander
¼ teaspoon salt
½ teaspoon pepper
¼ cup almond flour

Ingredients for Sandwich

1 English cucumber (¾ cup spiralized)
1 medium red onion (½ cup spiralized)
3 whole-wheat pitas
½ cup chopped tomatoes

Ingredients for Lemon Tahini Sauce

2 tablespoons tahini
1 clove garlic, minced
Juice of 1 lemon
1 tablespoon olive oil

1   Preheat oven to 400°F. Begin by preparing falafel patties. In a food processor or blender, blend together chickpeas, walnuts, garlic, parsley, cilantro, 2 tablespoons lemon juice, 2 tablespoons olive oil, cumin, coriander, salt, and pepper. You may have to blend several times, using a spoon to move around mixture.

2   Heat 1 tablespoon olive oil in a large pan on medium heat. Form chickpea dough into little patties and roll in the almond flour. Place into the pan and slightly press down on the top of the patties with a spatula to flatten. Cook for 1–2 minutes on each side, then transfer to an aluminum-foil-lined baking sheet. Bake for 15 minutes, flip the patties, then bake for an additional 15 minutes.

3   While falafel patties are cooking, cut cucumber in half crosswise and slice off both ends. Spiralize using the straight-noodle blade so cucumber comes out in waves. Remove excess moisture from cucumbers by pressing noodles lightly between two paper towels.

4   Peel off the first layer of the red onion and cut off both ends. Spiralize using the small-noodle blade. Cut pita bread in half, making a slice in each half to form a pocket. Evenly distribute cucumber, onions, and tomatoes.

5   Prepare tahini sauce by blending together tahini, garlic, lemon, and olive oil. When falafels are finished, add to pita and top with tahini sauce.

Minestrone Soup

A big bowl of soup can be soothing and nourishing, and on days that I feel like I need a bit of comfort or a nutritional boost, minestrone is always a good choice. Filled with vegetables and herbs, minestrone soup is an easy-to-prepare soup that contains an abundance of different vitamins and minerals, which can be especially essential if you are feeling under the weather. This soup is also so high in fiber, you'll be sure to feel nice and full after just one bowl—although there's no good reason why you shouldn't have more!

Serves 4

- 1 medium onion
- 4 cloves garlic
- 2 stalks celery
- 2 jumbo carrots
- 2 tablespoons olive oil
- ½ teaspoon oregano
- ½ teaspoon basil
- ¼ cup chopped fresh parsley
- 4 cups fresh spinach
- 1 (14.5-ounce) can diced tomatoes
- 4 cups vegetable broth
- 1 (15-ounce) can kidney beans, rinsed and drained

1 Chop onions, garlic, and celery. Slice off both ends of the carrots and spiralize using a small-noodle blade.

2 Heat 2 tablespoons olive oil in a large pot on medium heat. Add garlic and onions and cook for 5 minutes. Then add celery and carrots and cook for an additional 3–4 minutes. Add oregano, basil, parsley, and spinach. Cook for about 2 minutes until spinach has begun to wilt.

3 Add tomatoes and vegetable broth and bring to a boil. Reduce to a simmer, cover, and cook for 15 minutes. Add kidney beans and cook for another 15 minutes. Serve warm.

Collard Green Hummus Wrap

Wraps are a fun alternative to your typical bread sandwich, but they're still filled with excess flour, and sometimes even sugar. To solve this, instead of using a tortilla as your wrap, you can use a collard green. All you have to do is look for a large-sized collard green and soften it by steaming, which makes it even easier to roll. This vegan wrap is loaded with vegetables, which are held together by a homemade hummus. If you're short on time, you can use store-bought hummus, but it's quite simple to make your own and tastes much fresher when you do it yourself.

Makes 2 wraps

2 collard green leaves
1 cup canned chickpeas,
    rinsed and drained
1 clove garlic
1 tablespoon tahini
Juice of ½ lemon
1 tablespoon extra-virgin
    olive oil
½ medium avocado
½ large red bell pepper
½ medium cucumber

Get Creative with Your Hummus
You don't have to stick to plain hummus in your wraps. Add some sun-dried tomato, extra garlic, or red pepper to switch up your hummus flavors.

1   Boil a pot of water. Once it reaches a boil, hold your collard green over the steam for 1–2 minutes until leaf begins to soften. Place leaf on a cutting board and, moving horizontally, slice off the thick end of the stalk.

2   To prepare hummus, add chickpeas, garlic, tahini, lemon juice, and olive oil to a blender or food processor and blend until smooth. Add more olive oil as needed. Spread hummus along the middle of each collard green leaf.

3   Dice avocado and red pepper and sprinkle over hummus. Cut off both ends of your cucumber half and spiralize using a small-noodle blade. Press between two paper towels to soak out excess moisture. Top avocado and red pepper with noodles.

4   Pull the top of the collard green over vegetable mixture, tucking it underneath. Tuck in both the right and left ends of the green and roll from the top, keeping the sides folded in as you roll. Once collard wrap is fully rolled, cut in half down the middle and secure with toothpicks if needed.

Hearty Chicken Parsnip Noodle Soup

Growing up, my mom and grandma always made chicken soup that not only left me full but warmed my soul. There is just something so soothing about a bowl of chicken soup, and considering it does have healing effects, it's the perfect healthy comfort food. Using parsnip instead of noodles is a great solution to ditching the refined carbs, especially since many traditional soup recipes already call for parsnips. This is a quick-cook recipe that is brimming with flavor, perfect for a cool day or when you're feeling a bit under the weather.

Serves 4-6

- 1 large parsnip (about 2 cups spiralized)
- 1 medium onion
- 4 cloves garlic
- 2 tablespoons olive oil
- 4 carrots (about 1 cup chopped)
- 4 stalks celery (about 1 cup chopped)
- 1 pound free-range boneless, skinless chicken breasts
- 1 quart chicken broth
- 3 sprigs fresh thyme
- ¼ cup chopped parsley

1 Peel parsnip, cut in half crosswise, and slice off both ends. Spiralize using a small-noodle blade.

2 Chop onion and garlic. In a large pot, heat 2 tablespoons olive oil on medium heat. Add onion and garlic and cook for 3–4 minutes.

3 While onion and garlic are cooking, chop carrots and celery. Add to pot, stirring in with garlic and onions. Cook for 2–3 minutes. Mix in spiralized parsnips.

4 Add whole chicken breasts to pot along with chicken broth and thyme. Stir together and bring to a boil. Reduce to a simmer, cover, and cook for 30 minutes. Remove chicken breasts and cut into pieces. Return to pot.

5 When ready to serve, top with chopped parsley. Serve warm.

Veggie Sweet Potato Bun Sandwich

Vegetable-filled sandwiches can taste light and delicious, but sometimes they're not filled with balanced nutrients, leaving you feeling hungry not long after eating them. This sandwich solves that problem by using fiber-filled sweet potatoes instead of bread, and adding in smashed white beans as protein. Making sweet potato buns is quick and easy, and you can use them on any type of sandwich. You can also experiment with other vegetable buns to see which one is your favorite.

Makes 1 sandwich

1 large sweet potato

2½ tablespoons extra-virgin olive oil, divided

2 large cage-free eggs

2 tablespoons almond flour

1 tablespoon goat cheese

1 cup widely chopped kale leaves

2 basil leaves

½ cup canned white beans, rinsed and drained

¼ cup sun-dried tomato halves

1 Peel sweet potato, cut in half crosswise, and slice off both ends. Spiralize using a small-noodle blade. Heat 1 tablespoon olive oil in a large pan on medium heat. Add sweet potatoes, cover, and cook for 7–9 minutes.

2 Remove sweet potatoes from pan and add to a large bowl. Mix in eggs and almond flour. Spread sweet potato mixture onto a plate or cutting board, pressing the top flat. Using a ramekin like a cookie cutter, press down onto mixture to create circle-sized buns.

3 Heat 1 tablespoon olive oil in the pan on medium-high heat. Using a spatula, transfer sweet potato cutouts to pan, using the spatula and ramekin to reshape as needed. Cook for 5 minutes on each side, adding more olive oil if needed.

4 Remove sweet potatoes and press lightly between two paper towels, soaking up the excess oil. On one of the buns, spread goat cheese on top, creating the bottom half of your sandwich. Heat ½ tablespoon olive oil on medium heat in a small pan, add kale, and sauté for 3–4 minutes. Add on top of goat-cheese-covered bun along with basil leaves.

5 Place white beans in a small bowl and mash with a fork. Add to sandwich, top with sun-dried tomato halves, and cover with remaining bun.

Carrot Ginger Soup

Soup is delicious and easy to make, but it can also have some powerful health effects. This creamy and slightly spiced soup is filled with antioxidants, anti-inflammatories, and immune-system-boosting foods. Aside from the powerful carotenoids found in carrots, the soup also contains ginger, which can help alleviate stomachaches and strengthen your immune system, along with garlic and turmeric, which can also keep you energetic and free of disease.

Serves 4

6 medium or large carrots

2 tablespoons extra-virgin olive oil, divided

1 medium onion

4 cloves garlic

2" piece of ginger, grated

4 cups vegetable broth

1 teaspoon cinnamon

½ teaspoon turmeric

Optional: parsley, for garnish

1 Preheat oven to 425°F. Spiralize carrots using a small-noodle blade. Set aside 4 of the spiralized carrots for the soup and use 2 to roast for the topping. Put the noodles of those 2 spiralized carrots on an aluminum-foil-lined baking sheet and drizzle with 1 tablespoon olive oil. Roast for 10–15 minutes or until carrots begin to soften.

2 Chop onion and garlic. In a large pot, heat 1 tablespoon olive oil on medium heat. Add onion, garlic, and ginger and cook for 3–4 minutes. Then add remaining carrot noodles and cook for another 5 minutes.

3 Add broth to pot along with cinnamon and turmeric. Bring to a boil, cover, lower heat, and simmer for 30 minutes. Once soup has finished cooking, let slightly cool and then blend so soup is smooth. Top with roasted carrots and parsley and serve warm.

Moqueca with Plantain Rice

Moqueca is a Brazilian stew typically cooked with white fish in a coconut base. It is usually served with onion-and-garlic-filled Brazilian rice, but in this recipe we substitute white rice with plantain rice, which happens to fit in well with the stew's South American flavors. This version just calls for white fish, but you can also make it heartier by adding in shrimp or crab. Although I used olive oil in this recipe, you can also use palm oil, which is more traditional.

Serves 2–4

2 tablespoons extra-virgin olive oil, divided

1 medium white fish fillet

1 medium onion

4 cloves garlic

1 large tomato

1 cup vegetable broth

1 cup coconut milk

½ teaspoon red chili flakes

2 tablespoons chopped cilantro

Lime, to taste

Ingredients for Brazilian Plantain Rice

2 large plantains

½ medium onion

2 cloves garlic

1 tablespoon extra-virgin olive oil

⅓ cup vegetable broth

Salt

Pepper

1 Heat 1 tablespoon olive oil in a small pan on medium heat. Add white fish and cook for 3–4 minutes on each side. Set aside.

2 Chop onions, garlic, and tomatoes. In a large pot, heat 1 tablespoon olive oil. Add garlic and onions and cook for 5 minutes. Add tomatoes and cook for an additional 3 minutes. Add broth, coconut milk, and red chili flakes and stir everything together. Add fish, breaking it up into pieces in the soup. Bring to a boil and then reduce to a simmer for 10–15 minutes.

3 While soup is cooking, prepare Brazilian Plantain Rice. Peel plantains, cut in half crosswise, and slice off both ends. Spiralize using a small-noodle blade. You can choose to put noodles in a food processor and pulse into rice or chop with a knife, or you can put noodles into the pan and break pieces up using a spatula.

4 Chop onions and garlic. Heat 1 tablespoon olive oil in a medium pan on medium heat. Add onions and garlic and cook for 3–4 minutes. Add plantains, breaking into small pieces of rice if you haven't already. Cook for 2 minutes, then add vegetable broth. Cook for an additional 2–3 minutes and then season with salt and pepper.

5 Remove soup from heat and add plantain rice. Mix together, and top with cilantro and lime. Serve warm.

CHAPTER SIX
Snacks and Appetizers

Potato-Crust Pesto Pizza with Avocado

It's hard to come across someone who doesn't like pizza, but the delicious combination of white bread and cheese isn't the ideal choice for people who like to eat healthy. Although it might sound blasphemous, this pizza contains no bread and no cheese, but it will still have you drooling over a slice, as its crust is made out of crispy potatoes, and toppings include a flavorful kale pesto, fresh tomatoes, zucchini, and Italian herbs. All you need is a spiralizer, an oven-safe pan, and a hearty appetite to enjoy this healthified pizza that not only looks and tastes great but is vegan, gluten-free, and brimming with nutrients.

Serves 1 or 2 (makes 1 pizza)

Ingredients for Crust
1 large russet potato
1 tablespoon coconut oil
1 tablespoon almond flour
1 tablespoon flaxseed meal
1 tablespoon olive oil, plus more for drizzling

Ingredients for Kale Pesto
½ cup kale
1½ tablespoons walnuts
1 clove garlic
1 tablespoon olive oil
Juice of 1 small lemon

Ingredients for Toppings
½ zucchini, uncut
1 small heirloom beefsteak tomato
½ avocado
4 or 5 basil leaves
Olive oil, for drizzling
Oregano
Pepper

1 Preheat oven to 425°F. Peel potato, cut in half crosswise, and slice off both ends. Spiralize using the small-noodle blade. Toss with coconut oil, almond flour, and flaxseed meal.

2 Heat an oven-safe pan with 1 tablespoon olive oil on medium heat. Add noodles to the pan; form into a circular shape and pat down with a spatula. Cover and cook for 3–4 minutes.

3 Remove pan and place it in the oven; cook for about 10 minutes until potato crust is solid enough to transfer to a baking sheet. It may not be completely crisp and firm yet, which is okay. It just needs to stay together so you can continue to cook it on the baking sheet.

4 While potato crust is cooking, add kale, walnuts, garlic, 1 tablespoon olive oil, and lemon juice to a blender or food processor and blend together. Set aside. When potato crust has cooked for 10 minutes, remove from oven and drizzle with olive oil; bake for another 10–20 minutes or until crust is almost crispy.

5 Remove crust from oven and turn up oven temperature to 475°F. Using a peeler, create zucchini ribbons by dragging peeler from top of the zucchini to the bottom. You'll need about 5 zucchini ribbons. Thinly slice tomatoes and dice avocado.

6 Spread pesto over crust. Place basil leaves on top of pesto and then top with tomato, zucchini, and avocado. Bake for about 7–10 minutes or until veggies are cooked.

7 Remove pizza from oven. Drizzle with olive oil and a dash of oregano and pepper. Serve warm.

Sweet and Salty Apple Chips

These apple snacks have all the crunch of potato chips minus the fat from deep-frying and all that added sodium. Kids and adults alike will be impressed by the crispness of these chips, and a dash of salt with coconut sugar adds a little bit of sweet and saltiness, making these chips a little bit more interesting. Bake time for these chips is 2 hours, so make sure you set aside time to prepare these chips before enjoying them. It might also help to spray the parchment paper with nonstick spray before you put the apples on to prevent sticking.

Serves 3 or 4

2 medium apples
1 tablespoon coconut sugar
¼ teaspoon sea salt

If You Don't Have a Straight-Noodle Blade

Unfortunately, regular noodle blades won't work for these chips—you need the apples to be in slices, not noodles. If you don't have the correct blade, use a mandoline or cut chips by hand, slicing as thinly as you can.

1 Preheat oven to 225°F. Spiralize apples using the straight-noodle blade. Place apples on a baking sheet lined with parchment paper. Make sure they are placed flat and spread evenly or they won't bake properly. Top with sugar and salt.

2 Bake for 1 hour, flip apples, then bake for an additional 1 hour. Remove from oven and let cool for 1 hour to allow chips to get crispy.

Salt and Vinegar Sweet Potato Chips

Although the flavor of salt and vinegar chips is often intense and tangy, it's that exact reason why so many people are fans of the snack food. These savory chips are made using sweet potatoes, and are baked, not fried, making them a much healthier option than your traditional bagged version. It's important to use malt vinegar here, as other types of vinegar won't give you that traditional potato chip flavor. You also may have to cook your chips in batches; you want to make sure the sweet potatoes are evenly layered to attain ideal crispiness.

Serves 4

2 large sweet potatoes
½ cup malt vinegar
Nonstick cooking spray
2 teaspoons salt

1 Preheat oven to 375°F. Cut sweet potatoes in half crosswise and slice off both ends of each potato. Spiralize using a straight-noodle blade so sweet potatoes come out in thin slices. Put slices into a large bowl and cover with malt vinegar. Transfer contents of bowl to a large ziplock bag and refrigerate for 15 minutes.

2 Once sweet potatoes have marinated in vinegar, spray an aluminum-foil-lined baking sheet with nonstick cooking spray. Spread sweet potatoes evenly on a baking sheet (you may need two sheets). Sprinkle sweet potatoes with salt. Bake for 15 minutes and then flip chips over. Bake for an additional 18 minutes or until potatoes are crispy. Let cool for 15 minutes and then serve.

Zucchini Caprese with Burrata

Unlike many other types of salad, caprese is a traditional Italian salad that isn't chopped and tossed together with dressing but is instead sliced and stacked. This variation of the salad includes zucchini, which provides an additional base to the standard ingredients of tomatoes, cheese, and basil. Burrata cheese differs from other types of mozzarella such as buffalo mozzarella because it is filled with a creamy mixture, making it an extremely rich and decadent choice for the salad that pairs well with the lushness of the thick-ribboned zucchini noodles.

Serves 2–4

- 1 large zucchini
- 7 medium vine-ripened tomatoes
- 16 ounces burrata cheese
- ½ tablespoon extra-virgin olive oil
- ½ tablespoon balsamic vinegar
- ½ teaspoon oregano
- ½ teaspoon pepper

1 Cut zucchini in half crosswise and slice off both ends. Spiralize using a straight-noodle blade so zucchini comes out in ribbons. Evenly spread zucchini on a plate or platter and press flat.

2 Slice tomatoes in half and place on top of zucchini, making sure the cut side of the tomato is facing up so the burrata can sit above it.

3 Slice burrata into pieces just a little smaller than tomatoes and top each tomato with a piece. Drizzle with olive oil and vinegar and top with oregano and pepper.

Baked Parsnip Fritters with Avocado Cilantro Sauce

Parsnips are root vegetables that have a similar taste to potato, but you don't see them used as frequently in recipes as their more popular counterpart. However, just because they aren't the most popular vegetable doesn't mean they can't be made into a tasty little appetizer. Although fritters are usually fried, these are baked in the oven, which helps cut down on fat content. When you first bake your fritters, you may find that they don't bind together as tightly as you want them to—don't worry, after their first round in the oven, they will be stuck together in no time.

Makes about 8 fritters

1 large parsnip
2 large cage-free eggs
⅛ cup whole-wheat flour
⅛ cup bread crumbs
½ teaspoon garlic powder

Ingredients for Avocado Cilantro Sauce

1 medium avocado
1 teaspoon garlic powder
1 cup chopped cilantro
2 tablespoons apple cider vinegar
2 tablespoons extra-virgin olive oil

1 Preheat oven to 425°F. Peel parsnip, cut in half, and slice off both ends. Spiralize using a small-noodle blade. Use a knife to break up long noodles. Transfer to a large bowl.

2 Crack eggs in a medium bowl and lightly beat. Add flour, bread crumbs, and garlic powder and mix well. Pour over parsnip noodles and mix with your hands until noodles are evenly covered.

3 Form patties using your hands and place onto a baking sheet lined with aluminum foil. Keep patties stuck together by using your hands—they will solidify when baked. Bake for 15 minutes and then flip fritters over using a spatula. Bake for another 10 minutes or until crispy.

4 To make Avocado Cilantro Sauce, add all ingredients to a blender or food processor and blend until smooth. Serve a dollop on each fritter.

Guacamole with Pineapple and Jicama

Guacamole is quite good on its own, but if you want to switch up the classic dip and really impress your friends, try adding some pineapple and jicama, which adds a little sweetness and a bit of crunch. This tropical spin on guacamole tastes great with chips, in a sandwich, or even in a taco or burrito. If you prefer your guacamole spicier, you can add a whole jalapeño rather than half.

Serves 4–6

4 medium ripe avocados
½ jalapeño, finely chopped
⅓ cup chopped cilantro
⅓ cup chopped red onion
⅓ cup chopped cherry tomatoes
Juice of 2 limes
1 teaspoon garlic powder
1 medium jicama (¼ cup spiralized)
¼ cup chopped pineapple

1 Scoop avocado out with a fork and mash until there are no big chunks left. Add jalapeño and cilantro to avocado along with red onion and cherry tomatoes. Mix until ingredients are evenly combined into the avocado. Add lime juice and garlic powder, mixing evenly.

2 Peel jicama so outer skin is removed and slice off both ends. Spiralize using a small-noodle blade. Top guacamole with jicama and pineapple and serve immediately.

Preparing Your Guac Ahead of Time?
To prevent your guacamole from browning, squeeze a bit of lemon juice over the top, which will help preserve the avocado. Keep in the refrigerator for optimal freshness.

Cucumber Salmon Hand Rolls

Making sushi at home sounds like an extremely daunting task, but temaki, also known as hand rolls, are a great choice for beginners. All you have to do is pick your fillings, lay them on a sheet of seaweed, and roll away. With a little practice, you'll have it down like magic. Spiralized vegetables are great fillings for these hand rolls, especially cucumber. You can also choose to fill your temaki with other spiralized vegetables such as carrot, daikon radish, or even something more offbeat like squash.

Makes 6 hand rolls

3 sheets nori (seaweed)
1 cup cooked quinoa
¼ cup rice vinegar
½ English cucumber
½ pound salmon sashimi
½ medium avocado
1 lemon
Optional: sriracha hot sauce

Tips for Rolling Hand Rolls
Although hand rolls are the simplest type of sushi roll to prepare, they can take some practice. Make sure your hands are dry so you don't moisten seaweed. Place your fish diagonally, and tuck the end in when you roll diagonally. Practice makes perfect!

1 Split seaweed sheets in half lengthwise and lay flat with the shiny side down.

2 In a small bowl, combine quinoa and rice vinegar. Spoon about 1 tablespoon quinoa per hand roll and spread evenly on the left side of the seaweed sheet, which should be laying horizontally.

3 Cut off ends of cucumber and spiralize using a small-noodle blade. Soak up extra moisture from cucumber with a paper towel. Break up cucumbers with your fingers and evenly distribute to hand rolls, placing on top of quinoa.

4 Slice salmon sashimi evenly into 6 long pieces, then add to hand roll. Using a knife, remove avocado from its skin. Cut lengthwise into long slices. Add avocado slices on top of sashimi.

5 Take bottom left corner of seaweed paper and roll up diagonally so it forms a cone. Serve immediately with a squeeze of lemon juice on top of each hand roll. Top with sriracha if desired.

Avocado Zucchini Noodles

People love making pasta because it can be a super quick way to put together a meal. Just throw some sauce over some noodles, and voilà! When it comes to spiralized noodles, you can create the same types of dishes with just as much ease. In fact, some dishes you don't even need to heat. These zucchini noodles are raw and coated in a creamy avocado sauce, one you can whip up in just minutes. I promise you'll feel less guilty indulging in these noodles than you would going for your regular spaghetti with cream sauce.

Serves 2

2 medium zucchini
1 avocado
Juice of 1 lemon
10 cherry tomatoes, halved

1 Peel both zucchini. Slice them in half cross-wise and cut off both ends. Spiralize using a small-noodle blade.

2 Combine avocado and lemon juice in a small bowl and whisk until smooth. Toss noodles in avocado sauce and top with cherry tomatoes.

Caramelized Onion Dip

The spiralizer is great for quickly cutting onions, especially when you want them stringy, so why not take advantage of this use and make an onion dip? Instead of using sour cream, I use Greek yogurt for this dip, and there's no instant soup mix either—instead, real caramelized onions are used along with some garlic powder and Worcestershire sauce. The fuller fat the Greek yogurt, the creamier the dip will be, although any kind works well with this recipe.

Serves 4-6

1 jumbo yellow onion

2 tablespoons extra-virgin olive oil

Vegetable broth, as needed

2 cups Greek yogurt

3 teaspoons garlic powder

1½ tablespoons Worcestershire sauce

½ teaspoon pepper

¼ teaspoon salt

1 Peel onion and remove outer layer of skin. Spiralize using a small-noodle blade. Heat 2 tablespoons olive oil on medium heat. Add onions and cook for about 35–45 minutes until onions are caramelized. Check every 5 minutes and stir as needed. If onions begin to stick to bottom of pan and dry out, add a splash of vegetable broth as needed. Onions should be a warm brown color with a slightly sweet taste.

2 Lower heat to low and add yogurt, garlic powder, Worcestershire sauce, pepper, and salt. Mix in until yogurt is evenly combined with onions. Serve warm or at room temperature.

Butternut Squash, Dandelion, and Mushroom Flatbread

Flatbreads are a quick and easy way to put together a pizza-like dish without worrying about making dough or long baking times. You can add anything to your flatbread, but one of the benefits of flatbreads is you don't have to use the traditional pizza combination of tomato sauce and cheese, which makes flatbreads even more fun for vegetarians and vegans. Just begin with a base and top with all the vegetables you desire. This flatbread has a simple olive oil crust and uses the butternut squash as a base, but there is really no spiralized vegetable you can't use for this appetizer.

Makes 2 flatbreads

- 1 large butternut squash
- 2 tablespoons extra-virgin olive oil, divided
- 2 large whole-wheat pitas
- 1½ cups dandelion greens, stems cut off and greens cut in half
- 4 cloves garlic, sliced
- 2 tablespoons chopped sage
- 1 cup sliced cremini mushrooms
- Salt
- Pepper

1 Preheat oven to 400°F. Cut the bulbous end off your butternut squash and set aside. You will only be using the longer end to spiralize. Peel butternut squash until the top, tough surface is completely removed; then slice in half crosswise and cut off the remaining end. Spiralize using a small-noodle blade.

2 Place noodles on an aluminum-foil-lined baking sheet and drizzle with 1 tablespoon olive oil. Bake for 10 minutes.

3 Place 2 pita breads on a baking sheet. Brush with remaining 1 tablespoon olive oil. Divide squash noodles evenly and top pita breads with the squash. Cover with dandelion greens, sliced garlic, chopped sage, and sliced mushrooms. Drizzle with extra olive oil if desired. Top with a dash of salt and pepper. Bake for 10 minutes. Serve warm.

Substitutions for a Large Pita
If you can't find a large pita, you can use other types of bread for your flatbread base, including focaccia, grain tortillas, or lavash.

Pan-Fried Polenta with Pea Pesto and Radish

Polenta is a cornmeal-based dish that can be made into a porridge or baked, fried, or grilled into little cakes that are great as small bites. When pan-fried, they get crisper on the edges, and it becomes easy to top each little cake with anything from cheese to sauce and salsa to pesto. This version of polenta is topped with vegan pea pesto and spiralized raw radishes. Peas may sound unconventional for a pesto, but the addition makes the pesto creamy and rich, which helps complement the simplicity of the radish.

Serves 4–6 (makes 12 polenta cakes)

18 ounces precooked polenta
1 tablespoon extra-virgin
    olive oil
4–6 radishes
Salt
Pepper

Ingredients for Pea Pesto

1 cup frozen peas, defrosted
¼ cup shaved almonds
½ cup fresh basil
¼ cup mint
2 cloves garlic
2 tablespoons extra-virgin
    olive oil
Juice of 2 lemons

1 Slice polenta into little cakes, about ½" thick each. Heat 1 tablespoon olive oil in a large pan on medium-low heat. Fry polenta cakes in the pan for about 3–4 minutes on each side. Set cakes aside.

2 Cut off the ends of each radish. Spiralize using the large straight-noodle blade so that your radishes come out shaved. Depending on the size of your radish, some will come out curly and others will only produce little shavings. This is okay—both will work. Set aside spiralized radish in a bowl.

3 To make pesto, combine peas, almonds, basil, mint, garlic, olive oil, and lemon juice in a blender or food processor and blend until smooth.

4 Spread pesto evenly on top of each polenta cake. Top with a piece of radish on each polenta cake. Top with salt and pepper and a drizzle of olive oil if desired.

Grilled Polenta Cakes
If you have a grill, try throwing the polenta cakes on it instead of frying them for a crisper texture, and a great vegetarian addition to barbecues. Brush your polenta cakes with olive oil and grill for about 3 minutes on each side.

Jalapeño Sweet Potato Poppers

I'm a huge fan of spicy foods, so the thought of a hollowed-out jalapeño filled with different toppings sounds like a dream food to me. If you're worried about the heat, you'll be reassured to know that cooking jalapeños actually makes them more mild, and the dairy from the cheese and Greek yogurt in the filling can help balance out the spice from these poppers. Filled with spiralized sweet potatoes, these poppers take a bar food and make it much more unique and nutritious.

Serves 4

- 10 jalapeños
- 1 large sweet potato
- 1 tablespoon extra-virgin olive oil
- 1 cup Greek yogurt
- 1½ cups grated Cheddar cheese
- 4 stalks green onion

1 Preheat oven to 425°F. Slice jalapeños in half lengthwise and place on an aluminum-foil-lined baking sheet.

2 Peel sweet potato, cut in half crosswise, and slice off both ends. Spiralize using a small-noodle blade. Heat olive oil in a large pan on medium heat. Add sweet potatoes, cover, and cook for about 7–10 minutes or until sweet potatoes are soft. Break up noodles with a spatula. Add a scoop of noodles into the inside of each of the jalapeño halves.

3 In a small bowl, combine Greek yogurt and Cheddar cheese. Spoon mixture on top of sweet potato. Finely chop green onion and sprinkle over jalapeños. Bake for 20–30 minutes until jalapeños soften and cheese mixture begins to get slightly crispy on top.

Zucchini-Wrapped Dates

I have found that one of the most popular appetizers with guests is bacon-wrapped dates. There's something about that combination of sweet and savory, especially with the warm gooeyness of the dates. But bacon isn't the only thing you can wrap around a date—a wide spiralized zucchini makes a great healthy substitute for a piece of bacon. Spice up the vegetable with a bit of salt and pepper and you have another healthy starter that is sure to be just as much of a crowd pleaser.

Serves 4–6

2 cups Medjool dates
2 large zucchini
1 tablespoon raw wild honey
¼ teaspoon salt
¼ teaspoon pepper

1 Preheat oven to 425°F. Split dates in half and remove pits.

2 Slice zucchini in half crosswise and cut off both ends. Spiralize using a straight-noodle blade so noodles come out in thick ribbons.

3 Break the ribbons into 4"–5" pieces, brush both sides with honey, and wrap around each date 4 or 5 times. Secure with a toothpick, making sure it goes through zucchini on the top and bottom of the date. Place wrapped dates on a baking sheet.

4 Sprinkle with salt and pepper and bake for about 10–12 minutes. Serve warm.

Pear and Ricotta Crostini with Walnuts and Honey

If you're having guests over or hosting a party, crostini are great appetizers to serve that don't take a lot of time to prepare or cook. These are topped with spiralized pear and ricotta, and then drizzled with walnuts and honey for a little extra sweetness. This recipe includes instructions on how to make your own crostini, but if you are pressed for time, you can also use pre-made crostini or any small pieces of bread or crackers instead. Stick the finished crostini in the oven at 400°F for just a few minutes to serve them warm.

Serves 6 (makes 24 crostini)

- 1 baguette
- 4 tablespoons extra-virgin olive oil
- 1 pear
- ½ cup ricotta cheese
- 2 tablespoons wild honey
- ¼ cup finely chopped walnuts

1 Preheat oven to 350°F. Slice baguette crosswise into ¼"–½" slices. Brush both sides of bread with olive oil and place on a baking sheet. Bake for about 8 minutes on one side and then flip. Bake for another 4–7 minutes or until slightly golden.

2 While crostini are in the oven, spiralize pear using the straight-noodle blade so the pear comes out as ribbons or wedges. Place into a bowl and set aside.

3 When crostini are done baking, let cool for a few minutes. Then spread ricotta evenly onto one side of each piece. Top with a slice of pear on each.

4 Drizzle honey evenly over crostini and top with chopped walnuts.

Zucchini Veggie Tacos

Tacos are the perfect recipe for a light snack, but nothing feels worse than eating a greasy taco that leaves you feeling heavy and weighed down after chowing down. Since these tacos are meat- and dairy-free, they're light and refreshing, yet still filling thanks to the protein of the black beans and healthy fat from the avocado. They are dressed simply with lemon, so you don't have to worry about heavy sauces or too much cheese. If you want to add more heat into these tacos, just double the amount of jalapeño.

Serves 4 (makes 8 tacos)

- 2½ tablespoons extra-virgin olive oil, divided
- 8 soft yellow corn taco-style tortillas
- 2 avocados
- 2 medium zucchini
- 1 cup frozen corn, defrosted
- 1 (15-ounce) can black beans, rinsed and drained
- 1 jalapeño
- 1 tablespoon chopped cilantro
- 3 lemons

1 In a large pan, heat ½ tablespoon olive oil on medium heat. Add tortilla to pan and cook for about 2 minutes on each side until tortilla begins to puff up and turn golden. Repeat for remaining tortillas.

2 Scoop out avocado into a bowl and mash with a fork. Spread mashed avocado on each tortilla evenly, almost like you would spread sauce on a pizza. Set aside.

3 Cut zucchini in half crosswise and slice off both ends. Spiralize using a straight-noodle blade so they come out like ribbons.

4 Heat 1 tablespoon olive oil in a pan on medium-low heat. Sauté zucchini for about 2 minutes until ribbons are slightly soft. Evenly distribute zucchini onto each tortilla.

5 In a medium pan, heat 1 tablespoon olive oil on medium heat. Add corn; cover and cook for about 3–5 minutes until it's fully cooked. Evenly distribute corn onto each taco. Top with black beans.

6 Finely chop jalapeño and sprinkle onto each taco followed by cilantro. Complete tacos by squeezing lemon juice over each taco. Serve immediately so tortilla doesn't become soggy.

Sweet Potato Nachos

These nachos use spiralized sweet potatoes as chips. Unlike refined flour or corn-filled nachos, these are loaded with fiber and healthy antioxidants. If you like your nachos extra cheesy, you can double the amount of cheese you use. Same goes for the jalapeño if you prefer the dish to be spicy. If you also want the dish to be a bit more loaded and filled with extra protein, try adding in some shredded baked chicken, which turns these nachos more into an entrée.

Serves 2

- 1 large sweet potato
- 1½ tablespoons extra-virgin olive oil
- 1 cup canned black beans, rinsed and drained
- 2 tablespoons chopped yellow onions
- ½ cup chopped cherry tomatoes
- ½ jalapeño, sliced
- ½ cup Cheddar cheese or Mexican blend
- ½ avocado, diced
- Cilantro, for garnish

1 Preheat oven to 425°F. Cut sweet potato in half crosswise and slice off both ends. Spiralize using a straight-noodle blade so sweet potatoes come out in thin slices. Spread sweet potatoes on an aluminum-foil-lined baking sheet and drizzle with 1 tablespoon olive oil. Bake for 15–20 minutes or until sweet potatoes start to get crispy.

2 While sweet potatoes are cooking, chop onions, tomatoes, and jalapeño. In a large pan, heat ½ tablespoon olive oil on medium-low. Add black beans and onions and heat for 1–2 minutes until they become warm.

3 When sweet potatoes are ready, spread on a plate. Top with black beans and onions, along with cherry tomatoes and jalapeño slices. Sprinkle with cheese while plate is still warm, so it begins to melt. Finish off with diced avocado and a handful of cilantro to taste.

CHAPTER SEVEN
Beef and Pork Main Dishes

Down South Parsnip Noodles with Bacon and Collard Greens

Parsnips and bacon are often paired together, and many times they're prepared with pasta. Now you can skip the refined wheat while keeping together this timeless combo. The additional pairing of bacon and collard greens give this dish a Southern flair, making for a hearty, well-rounded dish that will have you craving these rich flavors no matter where you live.

Serves 2

2 large parsnips
2 large cloves garlic
½ medium onion
3 tablespoons extra-virgin olive oil, divided
2 cups collard greens
5 strips uncured applewood-smoked bacon
Optional: ¼ cup Parmesan cheese

1 Peel your parsnips, chop in half crosswise, and then slice off both ends. Spiralize using a small-noodle blade.

2 Finely chop garlic and onion. In a large pan, heat 1 tablespoon olive oil on low heat. Add garlic and cook for 1 minute, stirring. Then add collard greens and onions and cook for 3–4 minutes until greens are wilted and onions are translucent. Remove from pan and add to bowl; set aside for later.

3 In that same pan, heat 1 tablespoon olive oil on medium-low. Add parsnip noodles, cover, and cook for about 7 minutes, stirring every minute or two. Parsnips should be soft but not mushy.

4 In a separate small pan, heat 1 tablespoon olive oil on medium heat. Add bacon strips and cook for 3–4 minutes on each side until crispy, breaking up pieces so they are about 1" thick.

5 When parsnips are done cooking, add bacon, collard greens, garlic, and onion and toss. If you want more flavor, you can add the oil from the bacon pan to the noodles, tossing until evenly coated. Sprinkle Parmesan cheese on top if desired.

Zucchini Spaghetti and Meatballs

This version of spaghetti and meatballs nixes the processed carbohydrates of your typical spaghetti and uses zucchini instead. Make sure to soak up excess moisture from your zucchini before heating it up, or else it will be too watery when combined with the sauce. Cooking the zucchini a little less than you normally would will also help with the liquid problem, as will serving sauce on top of noodles rather than tossed.

Serves 4 (makes 14 meatballs)

Ingredients for Meatballs

1 pound grass-fed ground beef
1 large cage-free egg
1 tablespoon chopped parsley
1 tablespoon chopped garlic
½ cup bread crumbs
½ teaspoon red chili flakes
½ teaspoon oregano
½ teaspoon black pepper

Ingredients for Sauce

½ medium onion
3 cloves garlic
3 tablespoons extra-virgin olive oil, divided
1½ cans diced tomatoes (about 20 ounces)
1 tablespoon whole-wheat flour
1 teaspoon thyme
1 teaspoon oregano
1 teaspoon black pepper
½ cup grated Parmesan cheese

Ingredients for Noodles

6–8 medium zucchini
1 tablespoon extra-virgin olive oil

1 Preheat oven to 400°F. In a large bowl, combine beef, egg, parsley, garlic, bread crumbs, red chili flakes, oregano and black pepper. Using your hands, shape beef mixture into golf-ball-sized spheres and place onto an aluminum-foil-lined baking sheet. Bake for 15 minutes.

2 While meatballs are cooking, prepare sauce: Finely chop onions and garlic. Heat 1 tablespoon olive oil in a large pan on medium heat, add onions and garlic, and cook for about 2–3 minutes or until onions are translucent. Add tomatoes, whole-wheat flour, thyme, oregano, and black pepper. Bring to a boil and then reduce to a simmer. Cover and let cook for about 10 minutes. When sauce is finished, add 2 tablespoons olive oil and Parmesan cheese and mix well.

3 Cut zucchini in half crosswise and slice off both ends. Spiralize using a small-noodle blade. Heat 1 tablespoon olive oil in a large pan. Add noodles and cook for about 2 minutes until noodles are just beginning to get soft. Remove from heat. Sauce will help warm and soften noodles. Transfer noodles to a bowl and top with meatballs and sauce.

Slow-Cooked Pulled Pork over Plantain Rice

Pulled pork differs from normal pork in that it's much more tender, given that it's cooked for a long amount of time at low temperatures. This makes it easy to make in large batches without giving it much attention. Since classic pulled pork is often served over rice, it is a great complement to plantain rice, especially because it gives it a slightly Caribbean twist.

Serves 4

Ingredients for Pulled Pork
1½ pounds pork shoulder
¾ teaspoon cumin
½ teaspoon paprika
¼ teaspoon cinnamon
½ teaspoon Dijon mustard
1 tablespoon coconut sugar
½ medium onion
1 clove garlic
¼ cup chicken broth
¼ cup apple cider vinegar

Ingredients for Plantain Rice
3 large plantains
3 tablespoons extra-virgin olive oil
5 cloves garlic
1½ teaspoons cumin
½ teaspoon salt
½ teaspoon black pepper
1 cup chicken broth

1 Add pork to the bottom of your slow cooker. Mix together cumin, paprika, and cinnamon and rub onto the pork. Top with mustard and coconut sugar. Chop onion and garlic and add to slow cooker. Cover with chicken broth and apple vinegar cider and cook for 5 hours on high.

2 Remove pork from slow cooker and shred using two forks. Return shredded pork to slow cooker and cook on high for 10 more minutes.

3 To make Plantain Rice, cut plantains in half crosswise and slice off both ends. Spiralize using a small-noodle blade. You can choose to place noodles in a food processor and pulse into rice, or you can put noodles into the pan and break pieces up using a spatula.

4 In a large pan, heat olive oil on medium-low heat. Finely chop garlic and add to the pan; cook for 1 minute. Add plantains along with cumin, salt, and pepper. Cook for 2–3 minutes, breaking noodles into rice-sized pieces while plantains are cooking, if you haven't already.

5 Add chicken broth and bring to medium heat. Cook for about 4 minutes or until broth is absorbed. Top plantain rice with pork and serve warm.

Cheesy Chili over Sweet Potato Fries

Even as a healthy eater, I have my moments where I crave junk food. The trick to sticking to your good habits is taking those junk foods and making your own healthy version. This chili over sweet potato fries may seem like a late-night, indulgent diner snack, but it can actually be served as a meal! The spiralizer makes wonderful curly fries, and using sweet potato provides a fiber-filled base that's rich in antioxidants and vitamins. The chili is made with grass-fed meat and filled with spices that hold their own healing powers as well. Top it off with a little bit of cheese, and you have a guilt-free American classic that's in line with your clean-eating habits.

Serves 4

- 4 large sweet potatoes
- 4 tablespoons extra-virgin olive oil, divided
- ½ medium onion
- 2 large cloves garlic
- 1 pound grass-fed ground beef
- 1 (14.5-ounce) can diced tomatoes
- 2 tablespoons tomato paste
- 2 tablespoons chili powder
- 2 teaspoons cumin
- 1 teaspoon oregano
- 1 teaspoon red chili flakes
- ½ cup grated Cheddar cheese
- ½ cup chopped green onion

1 Preheat oven to 425°F. Cut sweet potatoes in half crosswise and then cut off both ends of each potato. Spiralize using a large-noodle blade. Place on a large baking sheet lined with aluminum foil and drizzle with 2 tablespoons olive oil. Bake for about 15–20 minutes or until edges of fries are crispy.

2 While potatoes are baking, begin preparing chili. Chop onions and garlic. Heat 2 table-spoons olive oil on medium-low heat and add onions and garlic; cook for about 3–4 minutes. Add meat and cook for about 4–5 minutes until brown. Add diced tomatoes and tomato paste and mix until absorbed into meat.

3 Reduce heat to low and mix in chili powder, cumin, oregano, and red chili flakes. Cover and cook for 15–20 minutes until beef mixture thickens, stirring every 5 minutes.

4 When potatoes are done, top with chili and then the cheese. The heat of the chili should melt the cheese within a few minutes. Top with green onion and serve warm.

Kale Chimichurri Steak with Roasted Cauliflower and Potato Noodles

This dinner plate combines the classic American comfort dish of steak and potatoes with the traditional sauce of Argentina, chimichurri. This version of chimichurri, however, has the addition of kale, giving it a nutritional boost while hardly affecting its taste. By serving the meat with cauliflower, you cut down on the amount of potato needed as well, boosting your intake of fiber and potassium. Cauliflower gets extremely soft when roasted, so its flavor blends especially well with the potato, making this trio a perfect substitute for your typical TV dinner, with a little Latin flair.

Serves 2

2 cups cauliflower florets

2 tablespoons extra-virgin olive oil, divided

2 (7½-ounce) organic New York strip steaks

½ tablespoon ghee (clarified butter)

1 large russet potato

Ingredients for Kale Chimichurri

3 cloves garlic

½ cup fresh parsley

½ cup kale

2 tablespoons dried oregano

½ tablespoon lemon juice

½ tablespoon white wine vinegar

1. Preheat oven to 450°F. Spread cauliflower florets onto an aluminum-foil-lined baking sheet and drizzle with 1 tablespoon olive oil. Bake for 15 minutes or until tops begin to turn golden.

2. If you have a separate oven, you can cook the meat while the cauliflower is roasting. If not, you can wait until it is finished. Preheat oven to 350°F. Spread ghee evenly over both pieces of meat and place on a baking sheet. Roast for about 30–35 minutes or until internal temperature of meat is 135°F.

3. While meat is roasting, prepare potato. Peel and cut in half crosswise and slice off both ends. Spiralize using a small-noodle blade. Heat a large pan on medium heat and add 1 tablespoon olive oil. Add potatoes and mix them around with a spatula so the oil coats them evenly. Cover and cook for about 8–10 minutes or until potatoes are soft.

4. To make Kale Chimichurri, blend garlic, parsley, kale, oregano, lemon juice, and vinegar in a blender or food processor until almost smooth but still slightly grainy. When steak and cauliflower are done roasting, add potatoes to a plate and top with steaks and cauliflower. Drizzle chimichurri over entire plate and serve warm.

White Sweet Potato Noodles with Prosciutto, Brussels Sprouts, and Dates

White sweet potatoes are the often neglected middle child of the potato family. Though we are used to using orange sweet potatoes in most dishes, white sweet potatoes are another fantastic option, especially when it comes to spiralizing. They are less sweet and more mild, making them a great option for replacing pasta in savory dishes. The Hannah sweet potato is one option for a white sweet potato, and its slightly sweet flavor plays well with both the savoriness of the prosciutto and sweetness of the chopped dates.

Serves 2

1 large white sweet potato

2½ tablespoons extra-virgin olive oil, divided

4 cloves garlic

3 tablespoons chopped shallots

2 cups shaved Brussels sprouts

¼ cup dates

6 ounces nitrite-free prosciutto

1 Peel sweet potato, cut in half crosswise, and slice off both ends. Spiralize using a small-noodle blade.

2 In a large pan, heat 1½ tablespoons olive oil on medium heat. Add noodles, cover, and cook for about 10 minutes or until noodles are slightly soft. Stir every 2–3 minutes to prevent bottom noodles from burning.

3 While noodles are cooking, chop garlic. In a separate medium-sized pan, heat 1 table-spoon olive oil on medium-low. Add garlic and shallots and cook for 1–2 minutes. Then turn heat to medium and add Brussels sprouts; cook for about 5 minutes until they are soft. Remove from heat.

4 Remove pits from dates and chop dates into bite-sized pieces. Add to Brussels sprouts pan and mix evenly. Transfer Brussels sprouts mixture to the pan with sweet potato noodles and toss until sweet potato is evenly coated. Break prosciutto into small pieces, and add to noodles. Season with salt and pepper if desired.

Can't Find White Sweet Potato?
If white sweet potatoes aren't accessible to you, you can use butternut squash noodles or golden beet noodles in this recipe instead. Regular potatoes may be too bland, and orange sweet potatoes may make the dish too sweet.

Butternut Squash Spaghetti with Slow-Cooked Bolognese

Anything home-cooked is always going to be tastier, more whole, and healthier, and the same is true for this version of Bolognese sauce. Though its flavor is close to the traditional style originating from Bologna, it uses grass-fed beef, making it a much better option for you than grocery store meat sauces. Instead of spaghetti, we use butternut squash, and the thick sturdiness of the squash noodles can handle the weight of the meat sauce. Slow-cooking the Bolognese really allows the meat to soften and marinate in its own juices, so be sure to give it the proper time needed to cook. Prepare the Bolognese in the morning or the night before to give the meat ample time to cook.

Serves 4–6

½ medium onion
1 jumbo carrot
1 stalk celery
4 cloves garlic
3 tablespoons extra-virgin olive oil, divided
4 tablespoons tomato paste
1 pound grass-fed ground beef
1 teaspoon fresh thyme
1 teaspoon dried oregano
Pinch of nutmeg
½ cup chicken broth
½ cup red wine
1 (14.5-ounce) can diced tomatoes
1 bay leaf
2 large butternut squashes

1 Finely chop onion, carrot, celery, and garlic. In a large pan, heat 1 tablespoon olive oil on medium-low heat. Add onion, carrot, and celery and cook for 5 minutes. Add garlic and tomato paste and cook for another 1–2 minutes.

2 Add beef and cook for 4–5 minutes until just browned. Add thyme, oregano, and nutmeg and stir until mixed evenly.

3 Add chicken broth and bring to a simmer for 10 minutes. Once chicken broth has been absorbed, add wine and simmer for an additional 10 minutes.

4 Transfer contents of the pan to a slow cooker. Add can of diced tomatoes and bay leaf and mix together. Cook on low for 7 hours.

5 To make squash noodles, cut the bulbous end off your butternut squash and set aside. You will be using the longer end to spiralize. Peel butternut squash until the top, tough surface is completely removed; then slice in half crosswise and cut off the remaining end. Spiralize using a small-noodle blade.

6 In a large pan, heat remaining 2 tablespoons olive oil on medium heat. Add squash, cover, and cook for about 10 minutes until squash is soft. Top with Bolognese sauce and serve.

Butternut Squash Noodles with Pumpkin Sage Sauce and Pork

This meal is best prepared in the fall and winter, as its main ingredient, squash, is at its peak during this time. This Pumpkin Sage Sauce is cream-free, but the combination of almond milk and nutritional yeast would have you think it's loaded with cream. If you don't like the taste of nutritional yeast or don't have any on hand, you can leave it out, and it won't affect your sauce.

Serves 4

2 large butternut squashes

3½ tablespoons extra-virgin olive oil, divided

2½-pounds boneless pork loin chops

¼ teaspoon salt

¼ teaspoon pepper

Ingredients for Pumpkin Sage Sauce

1 tablespoon extra-virgin olive oil

2 cloves garlic

½ medium onion

1 cup pure pumpkin purée

½ cup unsweetened almond milk

¼ cup nutritional yeast

¼ teaspoon salt

¼ teaspoon pepper

1 tablespoon ghee (clarified butter)

¼ cup chopped sage leaves

1   Cut the bulbous end off your butternut squash and set aside. You will be using the longer end to spiralize. Peel butternut squash until the top, tough surface is completely removed; then slice in half crosswise and cut off both ends. Spiralize using a small-noodle blade.

2   Heat 2 tablespoons olive oil in a large pan on medium heat. Add squash noodles, cover, and cook for about 7–10 minutes or until squash is soft. Remove from heat and set aside.

3   In a separate large pan or cast-iron skillet, heat 1½ tablespoons olive oil on medium heat. Add pork loin chops and season with salt and pepper. Cook for about 5 minutes on each side or until pork is no longer pink. Remove from pan and cut into bite-sized pieces. Add to butternut squash noodles.

4   In a small pan, heat 1 tablespoon olive oil on medium heat. Add garlic and onions and cook for about 5–7 minutes or until onions are very soft and browned.

5   To make sauce, combine pumpkin purée, cooked garlic and onions, almond milk, nutritional yeast, salt, and pepper in a blender or food processor and blend until creamy. In the small pan you used in the previous step, heat ghee on medium heat. Add sage leaves and cook for 3–4 minutes until they begin to crisp. Lower heat to low and add pumpkin mixture, mixing until sage becomes absorbed and the rest of the sauce begins to warm.

6   Pour sauce over squash noodles and pork, mixing until evenly coated. Turn heat on low if your noodles have gotten cold. Serve warm.

Beef and Broccoli Noodle Stir-Fry

Beef and broccoli noodles are an American takeout favorite, but they definitely don't scream out health food. These noodles use just the bare amount of ingredients—no fancy sauces, no added salt, and definitely no MSG. Using broccoli stems to make the noodles helps lighten your carbohydrate intake, and it allows you to use the whole broccoli, so you don't waste any food. After making this version of beef and broccoli, you'll probably never feel like you have to order take-out ever again.

Serves 4–6

- 1 pound organic skirt steak
- ½ cup plus 2 tablespoons soy sauce, divided
- 2 cloves garlic, chopped
- 1 tablespoon coconut sugar
- 3 tablespoons sesame oil, divided
- 4 stalks broccoli (need 4 stems and 2 heads)
- 3½ ounces shiitake mushrooms
- 1 red bell pepper
- 5 stalks green onion
- ⅓ cup raw cashews
- 2 tablespoons sesame seeds

1. Slice steak into thin slices. Place at the bottom of a baking dish. Combine ½ cup soy sauce, garlic, and coconut sugar. Pour over steak. Cover baking dish with plastic wrap and refrigerate for 1 hour.

2. Heat 1 tablespoon sesame oil in a cast-iron skillet or large pan on medium heat. Add steak slices and cook for 5 minutes on each side. Set aside.

3. Slice off broccoli heads from stems. Spiralize all 4 stems using a small-noodle blade. Keep 2 broccoli heads and set the others aside. Break florets into smaller pieces.

4. Heat 1 tablespoon sesame oil in a large pan on medium heat. Add broccoli noodles and florets. Cover and cook for 10 minutes.

5. While broccoli is cooking, chop mushrooms, red pepper, and green onion. In a separate pan, heat 1 tablespoon sesame oil on medium heat. Add mushrooms, red pepper, green onion, and cashews and cook for about 5 minutes.

6. When broccoli is done cooking, add steak and vegetable mixture, along with 2 tablespoons soy sauce and sesame seeds. Toss on low heat until everything is evenly coated and heated. Serve warm.

Pan-Seared Pork Chops with Apples and Onions over Garlic Greens

This meal is a great choice for people who follow the Paleo Diet, as it's a multifaceted dinner that doesn't include any refined grains. The pork is hearty and filling, and it's served over apples, onions, and greens, making it a balanced meal filled with fiber and other important nutrients and antioxidants. Any type of green will work here, so feel to use anything from kale to collard greens to Swiss chard, or even a blend if you choose. You can use bone-in pork chops or choose boneless; just be aware that using a piece of meat with the bone in will enhance its tenderness and flavor.

Serves 2

- 4 cloves garlic
- 3½ tablespoons extra-virgin olive oil, divided
- 4 cups leafy green of choice
- Salt
- Pepper
- 1 medium onion
- 1 apple
- 3 tablespoons apple cider vinegar
- 1 tablespoon ghee (clarified butter)
- 2½-pound organic pork loin chops

1. Finely chop garlic. In a large pan, heat 2 tablespoons olive oil on medium-low heat. Add garlic and cook for 1 minute. Then turn heat to medium and add greens, stirring until they are coated evenly with garlic and olive oil. Season with a dash of salt and pepper. Cook for about 7 minutes until greens are wilted. Turn off heat and set aside, or keep on very low heat to keep greens warm.

2. Chop up entire onion. In a large cast-iron skillet, heat 1½ tablespoons olive oil on medium-low heat. Add onions and cook for about 5 minutes, stirring occasionally. While onion is cooking, spiralize apple using a small-noodle blade. After onions have cooked for 5 minutes, add apple. Cook for another 5 minutes and then add apple cider vinegar. Cook for a final 5 more minutes on medium heat. Remove apples and onions from skillet and set aside in a bowl.

3. In the same skillet, add ghee. Add pork chops, seasoning with a dash of salt and pepper to taste. Cook for 5 minutes on each side or until pork is no longer pink on the inside. During the last minute, add onion and apple mixture to warm up in the pan.

4. Serve pork with apple and onions over garlic greens.

Golden Beet Sausage Pasta with Mushrooms and Parsley

Not everyone likes their pasta drenched in sauce, but every noodle dish needs a bit of heartiness and flavor. This beet pasta is the perfect solution to this. Since the golden beets are less earthy in flavor, their taste is accentuated by the garlicky combination of mushrooms and parsley, which provide a heartiness to the otherwise soft noodles. Throw in some pork sausage, and you have a dish that will not only keep your taste buds happy, but will leave you satisfied and full.

Serves 2

5 golden beets

3 tablespoons extra-virgin olive oil, divided

4 cloves garlic, chopped

1½ cups chopped cremini mushrooms

2 Italian pork sausages, sliced and then quartered

½ cup chopped parsley

¼ teaspoon salt

¼ teaspoon pepper

1 Preheat oven to 425°F. Peel beets and then chop off both ends. Spiralize using a small-noodle blade. Place noodles on an aluminum-foil-lined baking sheet and drizzle with 1 tablespoon olive oil. Bake for 15 minutes until beets are soft.

2 In a large pan, heat 2 tablespoons olive oil on medium-low heat. Add garlic and cook for 1 minute. Add mushrooms and cook for another 3–4 minutes until soft. Add sausage and cook for an additional 1 minute.

3 Remove from heat and add parsley and beets. Toss everything together and top with salt and pepper.

Turnip "Spaghetti" Carbonara

Of all the popular Italian pasta dishes that many people tend to love, spaghetti carbonara definitely falls on the unhealthy end of the spectrum. But make a few tweaks, and you can have a just as indulgent dish without any of the negative side effects. Here we use turnips instead of spaghetti, as turnips are firm and similar to spaghetti in texture and appearance, although it does add a much more peppery flavor. Traditional carbonara does call for cheese, but you can leave the Parmesan out if you're sensitive to dairy or looking to cut down on fat.

Serves 2

- 2 turnips
- 2 tablespoons extra-virgin olive oil, divided
- 3 strips uncured, nitrite-free bacon
- 2 cloves garlic
- 2 cage-free egg yolks
- ½ cup grated Parmesan cheese
- ½ teaspoon pepper
- 1 tablespoon chopped flat-leaf parsley

1 Peel turnips and slice off both ends. Spiralize using a small-noodle blade. In a large pan, heat 1 tablespoon olive oil on medium heat. Add turnips and cook for about 7–8 minutes or until turnip noodles are soft.

2 While turnips are cooking, heat 1 tablespoon olive oil in a separate pan on medium heat. Add bacon strips; cook for 5 minutes on both sides. While bacon is cooking, chop garlic. Once bacon is done cooking, remove from pan and lower heat to medium-low. Add garlic and cook for 1 minute. Remove garlic from pan and set aside. Chop bacon into small pieces. Add bacon pieces to turnip noodles.

3 In a small bowl, mix together egg yolks and Parmesan cheese. Reheat turnip noodles on medium-low until they just begin to warm. Add egg and cheese mixture and toss around noodles for 2–3 minutes or until egg is fully cooked.

4 Top with pepper and add parsley as a garnish. Serve noodles warm.

Potato Noodle Moussaka

One of the first Greek dishes I ever tried was moussaka, and it was hard not to get sucked into the cuisine after eating a creamy casserole of eggplant and minced meat. Although the Greeks don't typically use potatoes in their moussaka, it is traditional in the Balkan countries, which makes spiralized potato noodles a great addition to the entrée. Moussaka is usually topped with a rich béchamel sauce, but instead this recipe uses Greek yogurt and Parmesan cheese, which makes the casserole a little bit lighter.

Serves 4

- 1 medium eggplant
- 3 tablespoons extra-virgin olive oil, divided
- 2 large russet potatoes
- 1 medium yellow onion
- 2 cloves garlic
- 1 pound grass-fed ground beef
- 1 teaspoon cinnamon
- ½ teaspoon allspice
- ¼ teaspoon nutmeg
- ½ cup diced tomatoes
- 1 cup Greek yogurt
- ½ cup Parmesan cheese
- 2 cage-free egg yolks

1. Peel eggplant and cut into thin slices. Place on an aluminum-foil-lined baking sheet and drizzle with 1 tablespoon olive oil. Broil for 5 minutes and then flip and broil for another 8 minutes on the other side.

2. While eggplant is cooking, peel potatoes and cut in half crosswise; slice off both ends. Spiralize using a small-noodle blade. In a large pan, heat 1 tablespoon olive oil on medium heat. Add potatoes, cover, and cook for 7–8 minutes.

3. In a 3-quart baking dish, layer the bottom with potato noodles. Add a second layer with the eggplant.

4. Preheat oven to 350°F. To prepare the meat, chop onions and garlic. Heat 1 tablespoon olive oil in the pan on medium heat. Add onions and garlic and cook for 3–4 minutes. Add beef, cinnamon, allspice, and nutmeg and mix everything together. Cook until meat browns, about 5–7 minutes. Then add diced tomatoes, mixing in. Remove from pan and add as a layer above the eggplant in the baking pan.

5. Mix together Greek yogurt, Parmesan cheese, and egg yolks in a bowl. Spoon evenly over beef. Bake for 30–45 minutes until top is melted and slightly golden. Let cool slightly and serve warm.

Zucchini with Pork and Mushroom Ragù

Ragù is the generic Italian name for any meat sauce, and this particular sauce is made with chunky pork and mushrooms. If you prefer the sauce to be less tomato based and more meat filled, you can lessen the amount of crushed tomatoes. Since zucchini can get watery when mixed with sauce, it's best to slightly undercook the zucchini and then top with sauce when ragù is done rather than mix everything together first. This will keep your zucchini firm and the sauce from becoming diluted with water.

Serves 2 or 3

- 3 medium zucchini
- 4 tablespoons extra-virgin olive oil, divided
- 1 pound boneless pork shoulder
- Dash of salt and pepper
- 2 cloves garlic
- ½ large onion
- 1 cup chopped white mushrooms
- 1 cup crushed tomatoes
- ½ cup vegetable broth
- 1 sprig fresh rosemary
- 1 sprig fresh thyme

1 Cut zucchini in half crosswise and slice off both ends. Spiralize using a small-noodle blade. In a large pan, heat 1 tablespoon olive oil on medium heat. Add zucchini and cook for 3–4 minutes. Remove from heat and set aside.

2 Cut pork into small 1" cubes. Heat 2 tablespoons olive oil on medium heat in a large pan or skillet. Add pork and lightly season with salt and pepper. Cook for 5 minutes, flip pork, and cook for another 3–5 minutes. Set aside.

3 Chop garlic and onion. In another large pan, heat 1 tablespoon olive oil on medium heat. Add garlic, onions, and mushrooms and cook for 5 minutes. Then add crushed tomatoes, vegetable broth, rosemary, and thyme along with cooked pork. Reduce to medium-low heat, cover, and cook for 30 minutes.

4 When sauce is finished, remove rosemary and thyme sprigs. Transfer zucchini to bowls and cover with sauce. Serve warm.

Harissa and Lemon Yogurt Beef with Butternut Squash Noodles

If you're someone who pours hot sauce over everything, you'll enjoy cooking with harissa, a North African chili pepper paste. Combined with the fresh and spice-soothing flavor of the Lemon Yogurt Aioli, this dish is bursting with exotic flavors. This harissa is more on the mild side, but you can raise the heat by increasing the amount of cayenne pepper. If you're looking for more added fiber, you could even add some roasted chickpeas, which go along with the dish's North African influence.

Serves 2

1 large butternut squash
2 tablespoons extra-virgin olive oil, divided
½ pound grass-fed or organic stewing beef
Salt
Pepper
¼ cup beef, chicken, or vegetable broth

Ingredients for Harissa

2 cloves garlic
2 tablespoons tomato paste
1 tablespoon chili powder
1 tablespoon cumin
½ teaspoon paprika
½ teaspoon caraway
⅓ cup extra-virgin olive oil
1 tablespoon lemon juice

Ingredients for Lemon Yogurt Aioli

¼ cup Greek yogurt
2 tablespoons lemon juice
1 tablespoon extra-virgin olive oil

1. Preheat oven to 425°F. Cut the bulbous end off your butternut squash and set aside. You will only be using the longer end to spiralize. Peel butternut squash until the top, tough surface is completely removed; then slice in half crosswise and cut off both ends. Spiralize using a small-noodle blade. Place noodles on an aluminum-foil-lined baking sheet and drizzle with 1 tablespoon olive oil. Bake for 10–12 minutes.

2. While squash is cooking, prepare beef. Heat 1 tablespoon olive oil in a large pan or cast-iron skillet on medium heat. Add cubed beef and season with a dash of salt and pepper. Pour in broth and cook for about 3–4 minutes on each side. Remove from heat.

3. Prepare harissa by first finely chopping garlic until it forms a paste. You can sprinkle on a little bit of salt to help the garlic soften. In a small bowl, mix together tomato paste, garlic, chili powder, cumin, paprika, caraway, olive oil, and lemon juice until a smooth paste forms.

4. Prepare aioli by whisking together Greek yogurt, lemon juice, and olive oil until blended and smooth. In a bowl, top squash noodles with beef and drizzle with harissa and lemon aioli. Serve warm.

Balsamic Beef with Figs and Carrots

If you're not a fan of waiting around to slow-cook beef, this dish is for you. This quick-cook Balsamic Beef can be ready in just 30 minutes, and it hardly requires any preparation. The mix of balsamic vinegar and Worcestershire sauce makes for a flavorful and moist piece of meat, and the dish is slightly sweetened with the accompaniment of the carrots and figs.

Serves 2

2 cloves garlic

1 tablespoon extra-virgin olive oil

½ pound grass-fed Angus beef

6 small figs

½ cup balsamic vinegar

1 teaspoon Worcestershire sauce

1 teaspoon wild raw honey

3 sprigs rosemary

2 large carrots

Keeping Beef Moist

When placing beef in the oven, make sure it has been nicely coated in balsamic vinegar; this will keep it from drying out too much.

1 Preheat oven to 350°F. Finely chop garlic. In a large cast-iron skillet or oven-safe pan, heat olive oil on medium heat. Add garlic and cook for 1 minute. Add beef and cook for 30 seconds on each side. Remove from heat and add figs, balsamic vinegar, Worcestershire sauce, honey, and rosemary sprigs to skillet. Transfer skillet to oven and bake for 10 minutes. Flip beef and cook for an additional 10 minutes.

2 Fill a medium pot with water and bring to a boil. Cut carrots in half and slice off both ends. Spiralize using a small-noodle blade. Add carrots to boiling water and cook for about 5 minutes or until carrots begin to soften.

3 When beef is finished, serve over carrot noodles and use the remaining sauce in the pan to drizzle over dish.

CHAPTER EIGHT
Chicken Main Dishes

Mediterranean Golden Beets with Baked Chicken

Every time I travel to Mediterranean countries, one of the highlights of the trip is always food. I come home craving the light and fresh flavors of these coastal countries, and I'm always inspired to emulate the way they cook, especially because the Mediterranean diet has proven time and time again to be the healthiest way to eat. Golden beets are pretty neutral in flavor, so they go well with the vegetable-heavy influence of Mediterranean food with just a touch of cheese and chicken for added flavor and nutrients.

Serves 2

1 chicken breast

4 large golden beets

2 tablespoons and 2 teaspoons extra-virgin olive oil, divided

Optional: salt and pepper

12 cherry tomatoes, halved

1 large garlic clove, chopped

¼ cup chopped fresh mint leaves

¼ cup crumbled feta cheese

1　Prepare chicken first. Preheat oven to 350°F. Place chicken on a baking sheet on aluminum foil and cook for about 30 minutes. You can tell if chicken is cooked by slicing the inside and making sure it's not pink. Once chicken is done, remove from oven and turn oven up to 425°F.

2　Peel your beets and chop off both ends. Spiralize using a small-noodle blade. Put beets on an aluminum-foil-lined baking sheet, spreading evenly. Drizzle with 1 tablespoon olive oil and salt and pepper if desired. On a separate baking sheet, spread cherry tomatoes and drizzle with 1 teaspoon olive oil. Place both baking sheets in the oven and bake for about 20 minutes.

3　When beets and tomatoes are finished roasting, set aside. Heat 1 teaspoon olive oil in a large pan on low heat. Add garlic and cook for about 1 minute, then turn off heat. Add beets, tomatoes, mint, and feta cheese. Shred chicken using your fingers and add to pan. Toss with 1 tablespoon olive oil and serve warm.

Garlic Parsnip Noodles with Chicken

Garlic butter noodles: sounds like nothing but a heavy, indulgent dish. Thankfully, there's a way to make everything lighter and healthier, and this dish is no exception. These noodles use ghee, also known as clarified butter. It is commonly used in Asian cuisines and by people who are dairy intolerant, as ghee does not contain casein or lactose. The flavor is still rich and buttery, so it's a great substitute for regular butter or oil in many dishes.

Serves 2

2 large parsnips

2 tablespoons extra-virgin olive oil

3 tablespoons ghee (clarified butter)

3 tablespoons chopped garlic

½ cup chopped green onions

1 Peel parsnips and cut in half crosswise. Chop off ends and spiralize using a small-noodle blade. In a large pan, heat 2 tablespoons olive oil on medium heat. Add parsnips and mix around so they're evenly coated with olive oil. Cover and cook for 7–9 minutes until parsnips are very soft, stirring every 2 minutes or so. Turn off heat and set aside.

2 In a small pan, heat 3 tablespoons ghee on low heat. Add garlic and cook for 1 minute, making sure to stir it frequently so it doesn't burn. After 1 minute, turn off heat. Add garlic butter to parsnip noodles and toss. Top with green onion and serve warm.

White Sweet Potato Noodles with Spicy Arrabiata and Baked Chicken

Arrabiata sauce is a traditional Italian spicy tomato sauce, and it is actually a quite simple sauce to prepare. Adjust the heat of your sauce by adding or subtracting red chili flakes, although this recipe falls on the middle of the heat spectrum. Though arrabiata is frequently served with penne pasta, the thick starchiness of white sweet potatoes makes them a great substitute. If you want to spruce up your sauce, try adding in a sprinkle of parsley or Parmesan cheese.

Serves 4

- 1 pound large free-range boneless, skinless chicken breast
- 2 large white sweet potatoes
- 5 cloves garlic
- 8 tablespoons extra-virgin olive oil, divided
- 1 tablespoon red chili flakes
- ⅓ cup tomato paste
- 2 cups diced tomatoes
- ½ cup red wine
- ¼ teaspoon salt

1 Preheat oven to 350°F. Place chicken on an aluminum-foil-lined baking sheet and bake for 30 minutes.

2 Peel sweet potatoes and cut in half crosswise, then slice off both ends. Spiralize using a small-noodle blade. Set noodles aside to cook when sauce is ready.

3 Finely chop garlic cloves. Heat 4 tablespoons olive oil in a large pan on medium-low heat. Add garlic and red chili flakes, stirring around to prevent garlic from burning. Cook garlic and red chili flakes in olive oil for 5 minutes.

4 Add tomato paste and stir around for about 1 minute until it is coated in the oil. Stir in diced tomatoes and turn to medium heat. Add wine, bring to a boil, and cook for 2–3 minutes.

5 Reduce heat to low and cover sauce. Let simmer for 15–20 minutes. When sauce is finished, add 2 tablespoons olive oil and salt.

6 To cook sweet potatoes, heat 2 tablespoons olive oil in a large pan on medium heat. Add noodles, cover, and cook for about 10 minutes or until noodles are slightly soft.

7 While potatoes are cooking, cut chicken into strips and cut those strips in half. When potatoes are finished, add chicken to noodles and top with arrabiata sauce, tossing around until noodles are evenly coated.

Chicken Sweet Potato Enchilada Bake

An ooey, gooey enchilada is one of my favorite Mexican dishes. This lightened-up version uses sweet potato instead of tortilla and shredded chicken in place of beef. If you don't have a blend of cheeses, you can choose to just use Cheddar cheese and the taste will remain similar.

Serves 4

- 1 free-range boneless, skinless chicken breast
- 3 tablespoons vegetable oil
- 1 tablespoon whole-wheat flour
- ½ teaspoon cumin
- ¼ teaspoon oregano
- 3 tablespoons chili powder
- 1 cup tomato paste
- 2 cups chicken broth
- 1 tablespoon cayenne pepper hot sauce
- 2 medium sweet potatoes (2 cups spiralized)
- 1 jalapeño
- 1 cup canned black beans, rinsed and drained
- 1 cup Mexican-blend cheese
- 1 stalk green onion, sliced
- ½ avocado, diced
- ½ cup Greek yogurt

1 Preheat oven to 350°F. Bake chicken on an aluminum-foil-lined baking sheet for 25 minutes.

2 While chicken is baking, prepare enchilada sauce. In a medium saucepan, heat vegetable oil on medium heat. Add flour and stir until flour is evenly coated with oil. Then add cumin, oregano, and chili powder and stir until they are mixed evenly. Mix in tomato paste, chicken broth, and hot sauce; stir for about 2–3 minutes on medium heat until chunks are gone and mixture is smooth. Reduce to a simmer and cook for 15 minutes. The chicken broth should begin to dissolve and sauce will thicken.

3 Peel sweet potatoes, cut in half crosswise, then slice off both ends. Spiralize using a small-noodle blade. Grease the bottom of an 8" × 12" casserole dish and evenly layer sweet potatoes.

4 When chicken is finished and has cooled, shred using your fingers or two forks. Preheat oven to 400°F. Slice your jalapeño crosswise into ¼" slices and then finely chop. In a medium-sized bowl, combine chicken, black beans, jalapeño, and 1 cup enchilada sauce (you will have extra). Spoon mixture to evenly cover sweet potatoes.

5 Top enchilada with 1 cup cheese and cover with aluminum foil. Bake for 30 minutes, remove foil, and cook for another 10 minutes. Remove from oven and let cool. Top with sliced green onions and serve warm with a side of diced avocado, Greek yogurt, and extra enchilada sauce.

Chicken with Caramelized Onions, Mushrooms, and Spinach

Most of us have had caramelized onions, and if you've ever cooked them before, you know they require patience and observance. In this entrée, it's not just the onions that are caramelized. You can also do a similar process with mushrooms. Although they don't get as soft as onions, they take on a softer texture and a sweeter flavor that mixes well with caramelized onions. This recipe calls for chicken thighs, as they are a little richer and fattier, which works with this particular dish. However, you can also use chicken breasts here as well.

Serves 3

- 2 medium onions
- 6 tablespoons extra-virgin olive oil, divided
- Vegetable broth, as needed
- 3 cups sliced white mushrooms
- 1½ tablespoons Worcestershire sauce, divided
- Pepper, to taste
- 1 tablespoon balsamic vinegar
- 4 cloves garlic
- 1 (6-ounce) bag spinach leaves
- 1 pound free-range boneless chicken thighs
- Dash of coriander

1   Peel and cut off the ends of both onions and spiralize using a small-noodle blade. Heat 2 tablespoons olive oil in a cast-iron skillet or large pan on medium heat. Add onions and cook for about 35–45 minutes until onions are caramelized. Check every 5 minutes and stir as needed. If onions begin to stick to bottom of pan and dry out, add a splash of vegetable broth as needed. Onions should be a warm brown color with a slightly sweet taste.

2   In a separate pan, while onions are cooking, heat 2 tablespoons olive oil on medium heat. Add mushrooms, ½ tablespoon Worcestershire sauce, and pepper if desired. Cook for about 15–20 minutes until mushrooms begin to get very soft and brown. When mushrooms begin to dry out, about 10 minutes in, add balsamic vinegar to keep moist.

3   When mushrooms are done cooking, remove from pan. Chop garlic cloves. In the same pan or a separate pan, heat 1 tablespoon olive oil on medium-low heat. Add garlic and cook for 1–2 minutes. Then add spinach and cook for 3–5 minutes or until leaves are wilted. Remove from pan.

4   Slice chicken thighs in small strips. Heat 1 tablespoon olive oil on medium heat. Add chicken and remaining 1 tablespoon Worcestershire sauce and cook for 5–6 minutes on each side or until inside is fully cooked. When chicken and onions are complete, mix everything together and serve warm.

Moroccan Chicken with Spiralized Carrots and Chickpeas

The cuisine of Morocco is rich in spices, and it often mixes savory with sweet. Influenced by Middle Eastern and Mediterranean cuisine, Moroccan food also contains a wide variety of vegetables. This chicken is cooked in a honey sauce and served with boiled carrot noodles and spiced roasted chickpeas, giving it an exotic flair that will likely leave your mouth watering for more. If you don't have currants, you can use raisins in their place instead; the taste will be similar.

Serves 4

Ingredients for Roasted Chickpeas

1 (15-ounce) can chickpeas, rinsed and drained
1 tablespoon olive oil
½ teaspoon oregano
½ teaspoon cumin
¼ teaspoon pepper

Ingredients for Chicken

4 cloves garlic
½ tablespoon minced fresh ginger
¼ cup extra-virgin olive oil
½ teaspoon oregano
¼ teaspoon paprika
½ teaspoon cumin
¼ teaspoon turmeric
¼ teaspoon coriander
¼ teaspoon cinnamon
¼ cup currants
¼ cup shaved almonds
½ tablespoon honey
4 organic, free-range chicken drumsticks
3 jumbo carrots

1 Preheat oven to 425°F. Line a baking sheet with aluminum foil and spread chickpeas evenly. Drizzle with 1 tablespoon olive oil and sprinkle with oregano, cumin, and pepper. Bake for 20–30 minutes or until chickpeas get crispy.

2 While chickpeas are cooking, finely mince garlic. In a cast-iron skillet or large oven-safe pan, heat ¼ cup olive oil on medium-low heat. Add garlic and ginger and cook for about 2 minutes. Turn heat to low. Then add oregano, paprika, cumin, turmeric, coriander, and cinnamon, stirring around until spices are mixed.

3 Mix in currants, almonds, and honey. Add drumsticks and cook for 1–2 minutes, mixing drumsticks with spice mixture. Transfer pan to oven. Bake for 30 minutes or until chicken is white on the inside. While chicken is cooking, spiralize carrots. Slice off both ends of all the carrots, and spiralize using a small-noodle blade. Boil carrots for 3–4 minutes or until they begin to get soft. When chicken skillet is ready, serve over carrot noodles and top with roasted chickpeas.

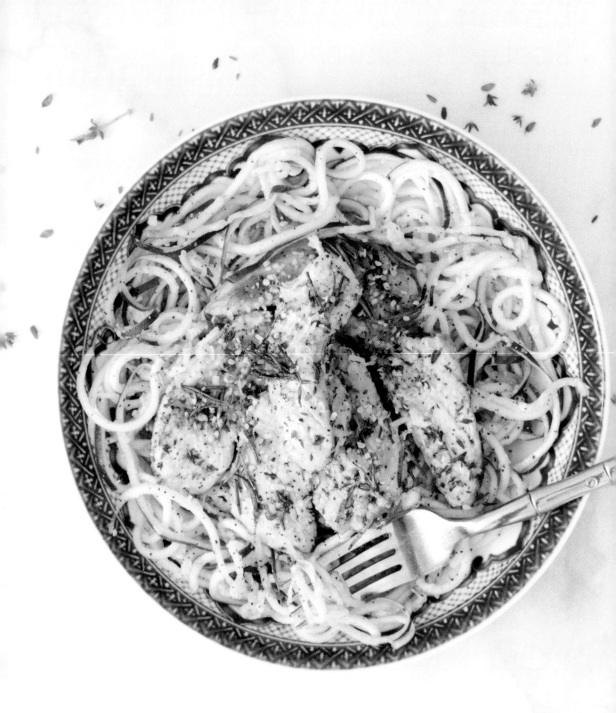

Lemon Zucchini Noodles with Herbed Chicken and Hemp Seeds

Some days you may be craving something healthy but don't want to spend too much time or money whipping up a fancy vegetable-filled dish. This noodle dish is made for one of those days, as it's a quick-cook pasta dressed simply with lemon and herbs. Throwing in some hemp seeds not only provides the dish with a little bit of extra protein and healthy omega-3 fatty acids, but it gives the dish more texture with the seeds' slight crunch. This recipe calls for thyme and rosemary, but you can use anything from dried parsley to oregano as well.

Serves 2

2 large zucchini
1½ tablespoons extra-virgin olive oil, divided
1 chicken breast
1 tablespoon dried rosemary
1 tablespoon dried thyme
1 tablespoon hemp seeds
Juice of 2 small lemons
Optional: Parmesan cheese

1 Cut zucchini in half crosswise and chop off both ends. Spiralize using the small-noodle blade. Pat down noodles with a paper towel to remove excess moisture.

2 Heat 1 tablespoon olive oil in a large pan on medium heat. Add zucchini noodles and cook for about 3–4 minutes, stirring noodles around so they cook evenly. Remove from heat.

3 In a small pan, heat ½ tablespoon olive oil on medium heat. Add chicken, rosemary, thyme, and hemp seeds and toss around until evenly coated. Cook for about 5 minutes then flip. Using a spatula, break chicken up into pieces so it cooks evenly. Cook for another 6–7 minutes or until inside is fully cooked.

4 Add chicken to zucchini and toss with lemon juice. Serve warm and add Parmesan cheese if desired.

White Carrot Noodles with Spinach, Roasted Red Pepper Sauce, and Chicken

This red pepper sauce is dairy-free, which makes this recipe great for those on the Paleo Diet. Though this recipe calls for white carrots, regular orange carrots can be used as well. Be sure to soak your cashews overnight to ensure that your sauce is smooth and creamy. Otherwise, the texture may end up being more thick and chunky like a pesto.

Serves 2

3 big white carrots (or 6 small)

¼ teaspoon salt

2 cloves garlic

¾ tablespoon ghee (clarified butter) or extra-virgin olive oil

4 cups uncooked spinach

1 free-range boneless, skinless chicken breast

1 tablespoon extra-virgin olive oil

Ingredients for Red Pepper Sauce

1 (12-ounce) jar roasted red peppers

2 cloves garlic

½ cup soaked cashews

½ cup coconut milk

1 tablespoon extra-virgin olive oil

1 Cut off the thin parts of the carrot; these won't be able to spiralize. Cut a slice off both ends of your carrot so the spiralizer has enough diameter to catch. Spiralize carrots, using a small-noodle blade, adjusting the spiralizer to their curves if needed.

2 Fill a medium-sized pot with water and ¼ teaspoon salt and bring to a boil. Add carrots and boil for 5–7 minutes. When carrots are finished, strain and set aside.

3 While carrots are cooking, chop garlic. In a small pan, heat ghee or olive oil on medium-low heat. Add garlic and spinach and cook for about 2 minutes until spinach is wilted. Remove from heat and set aside.

4 Prepare chicken by cutting into 1" cubes. In a medium pan, heat 1 tablespoon olive oil over medium heat. Add chicken to pan and cook for about 3–4 minutes on each side or until thoroughly cooked.

5 To prepare sauce, combine roasted red peppers, garlic, soaked cashews, coconut milk, and olive oil in a blender or food processor and blend until smooth. Transfer to a small saucepan and cook on medium heat until almost to a boil, stirring occasionally. Sauce should thicken.

6 Transfer carrot noodles to pan with chicken and add spinach mixture. Pour Red Pepper Sauce over contents of pan and mix evenly until noodles are thoroughly coated. Turn heat on low if you need to reheat the chicken and noodles. Serve warm.

Creamy Sun-Dried Tomato Zucchini with Chicken and Lentils

If you ever find yourself getting sick of regular tomato sauce, it's always a good option to cook with sun-dried tomatoes instead. They still contain all the nutrients of regular tomatoes, but they have a more potent taste than regular tomatoes, in the best way possible, of course. For this recipe, it's best to use sun-dried tomatoes from the jar, as they contain a flavorful oil that can enhance the sauce. However, if you don't have jarred tomatoes, you can just add regular olive oil, and you can also season the sauce with any additional spices such as oregano or basil that would typically come in a sun-dried tomato jar.

Serves 2

- 1 free-range boneless, skinless chicken breast
- 3 medium zucchini
- 5½ tablespoons extra-virgin olive oil, divided
- 6 tablespoons sun-dried tomatoes
- 2 cloves garlic
- ¼ cup Greek yogurt
- 3 teaspoons white wine vinegar
- ½ cup cooked lentils

1 Preheat oven to 350°F. Place chicken on a baking sheet and bake for 30 minutes. When chicken is finished baking and has cooled, cut into small pieces, either strips or cubes, for the pasta.

2 Cut zucchini in half crosswise and slice off both ends from each zucchini. Spiralize using a small-noodle blade. Heat 1½ tablespoons olive oil in a large pan on medium-low heat. Add zucchini noodles and cook for 3–4 minutes. Remove from heat.

3 To make sun-dried tomato sauce, add sun-dried tomatoes, garlic, 4 tablespoons olive oil (or oil from sun-dried-tomato jar), Greek yogurt, and white wine vinegar to a blender or food processor and blend until smooth. Add sauce to noodle pan on low heat, mixing in noodles with sauce to warm. Add lentils and chicken and serve warm.

Lemon Goat Cheese Turnip Noodles with Broccoli and Chicken

The taste of turnip can be strong, so why not make it a bit more mild by breaking it into smaller, noodle-sized bites and topping it with a creamy combination of goat cheese, broccoli, and chicken? This loaded dish is smothered in creamy lemon goat cheese and filled with nutrient-rich broccoli and pan-fried chicken. Goat cheese is easier on the digestive system than cow's milk cheese, which makes these noodles a good choice for people who are slightly sensitive to dairy.

Serves 2

2 medium turnips

3 tablespoons extra-virgin olive oil, divided

2 cloves garlic

1 head broccoli (about 1 cup broccoli florets)

1 free-range boneless, skinless chicken breast

¾ cup cherry tomatoes, halved

¼ cup chopped fresh basil

4 tablespoons goat cheese

Juice of 2 lemons

1 tablespoon bread crumbs

¼ teaspoon black pepper

1 Peel turnips and slice off both ends. Spiralize using a small-noodle blade. In a large pan, heat 1 tablespoon olive oil on medium heat. Add turnips and cook for about 7 minutes or until noodles begin to soften. Set aside.

2 Chop garlic. Heat 1 tablespoon olive oil on medium-low heat. Add garlic and cook for 1 minute. Turn heat to medium and add broccoli. Cover pan and cook for about 5 minutes until broccoli is soft.

3 While broccoli is cooking, slice chicken into thin strips. Heat 1 tablespoon olive oil in a small pan on medium heat. Add chicken strips and cook for 3 minutes on each side.

4 When broccoli is done cooking, add chicken, cherry tomatoes, basil, and turnip noodles. Toss together with goat cheese and lemon juice until evenly coated. Remove from heat and top with bread crumbs and black pepper.

Slow-Cooker Buffalo Chicken Lettuce Cups with Spiralized Carrots

Buffalo chicken is a staple in American cuisine, but it's not exactly your quintessential health food. Luckily, there's a way to lighten up anything. This version of Buffalo chicken is made with Greek yogurt and just a dash of blue cheese, keeping its rich flavor without all the saturated fat. The chicken is cooked in a slow cooker, making it juicy and extremely easy to shred. To make this Buffalo chicken even more healthy, it's enjoyed in a lettuce cup rather than on a piece of bread (though you always have that option if you want to take some leftovers on the go). Be sure to prepare the chicken the morning or night before so you have time to let it cook in the slow cooker.

Serves 3 or 4

- 1 pound free-range boneless, skinless chicken breasts
- ½ medium onion
- 2 cloves garlic
- 2 cups chicken broth
- ⅓ cup Greek yogurt
- 2 tablespoons crumbled blue cheese
- ½ cup cayenne pepper hot sauce (I used Frank's)
- 1 jumbo carrot
- 3 stalks green onion
- 6–8 leaves Bibb lettuce

1 Place chicken in your slow cooker. Chop onions and garlic and add on top of chicken. Pour chicken broth over contents of slow cooker and cover. Cook on high for 4 hours.

2 Once chicken is finished, remove from slow cooker. Shred chicken using two forks. Remove the broth from the slow cooker, saving ¾ cup to pour back over chicken. Add chicken back to the slow cooker and cover with broth you removed. Cook for 15 minutes on high.

3 While shredded chicken is cooking, whisk together Greek yogurt, blue cheese, and hot sauce to make Buffalo sauce. After chicken has cooked for 15 minutes, add Buffalo sauce and cook for another 15 minutes.

4 Cut off the small tail end of the carrot. Cut off both ends so there is enough surface area for the spiralizer to catch on to. Spiralize using a small-noodle blade. Trim noodles into smaller pieces and set aside. Finely chop green onion.

5 Once chicken is finished, scoop a generous amount of shredded chicken and place into a large leaf of lettuce. Top with carrots and green onion and enjoy immediately.

Zucchini Pad Thai

Pad thai has become a recent Thai-food favorite, but it actually has Chinese origins. That being said, Americans have created their own take on the street-style noodle dish, and many healthy foodies are now jumping in and making lighter visions of the noodles as well. This pad thai is made with zucchini noodles, and the sauce's base is made with almond butter, giving it a slightly different, but more healthy, taste than your traditional pad thai while still keeping all the essential elements of this world-famous dish.

Serves 2

3 zucchini

2 tablespoons coconut oil, divided

2 cloves garlic

3 stalks green onion

1 free-range boneless, skinless chicken breast, cut into strips

2 large cage-free eggs

¾ tablespoon raw almond butter

2 tablespoons soy sauce

2½ tablespoons fish sauce

1 tablespoon white wine vinegar

2 tablespoons coconut sugar

1 teaspoon red chili flakes

Juice of ½ lime

¼ cup shredded carrots

¼ cup mung bean sprouts

½ tablespoon crushed raw cashews

1 tablespoon chopped cilantro

1 Cut zucchini in half crosswise and slice off both ends. Spiralize using a small-noodle blade. Pat between two pieces of paper towel to take out excess moisture.

2 Heat 1 tablespoon coconut oil in a large pan on medium heat. Add zucchini noodles and cook for about 2 minutes until slightly soft. You want to leave them a little firmer than you think, as the warm sauce will help cook them down when added. Remove from heat and set aside.

3 In a medium pan, heat 1 tablespoon coconut oil on medium-low heat. Chop garlic and green onion; cut your green onion into long pieces but leave the ends for garnish. Finely chop the ends and set aside for later. Add remaining green onion and garlic to the pan and cook for about 1 minute. Add chicken strips and cook for about 3–4 minutes on each side or until chicken is thoroughly cooked. Don't worry about drying out the chicken; the sauce will help moisten it later on.

4 When chicken is almost done cooking, crack eggs into the pan. Let the eggs sit for about 30 seconds and then lightly scramble them all around until they are fully cooked. You don't want to the egg to be mixed and smooth—you want the yolk and whites to be somewhat separated and textured. Remove from heat.

5 To prepare sauce, mix almond butter, soy sauce, fish sauce, vinegar, coconut sugar, red chili flakes, and lime juice in a small bowl. Then add mixture to a small saucepan and heat until it comes to a low boil, stirring occasionally.

6 When sauce is finished, add chicken mixture to pan with noodles and top with sauce, tossing noodles until they are fully coated. Remove noodles and chicken from pan and place in a bowl, leaving excess sauce. Top with remaining green onion, carrots, bean sprouts, cashews, and cilantro. Serve immediately and with remaining sauce if desired.

Sweet Potato Noodles with Crispy Sage and Chicken

Lazy days in the kitchen are okay. In fact, sometimes the dishes that require the least effort can actually end up tasting the best. This noodle dish is made for one of those days. Just prepare the chicken in a slow cooker the night before, and you can throw together this noodle dish in just minutes. This dish also tastes delicious topped with Parmesan cheese, although it's not necessary.

Serves 2

1 free-range boneless, skinless chicken breast

1 tablespoon water

2 large sweet potatoes

2½ tablespoons extra-virgin olive oil, divided

4 cloves garlic

⅓ cup fresh sage

Salt

Pepper

1 Add chicken to the slow cooker with 1 tablespoon water. Cook on low for 8 hours. When chicken is finished, use fingers to shred chicken.

2 When you're ready to make sweet potato noodles, peel sweet potatoes, cut in half crosswise, and slice off both ends. Spiralize using a small-noodle blade. Heat 1 tablespoon olive oil in a large pan on medium heat. Add noodles, cover, and cook for about 7 minutes or until noodles are soft, stirring occasionally.

3 Finely chop garlic. In a small pan, heat 1½ tablespoons olive oil on medium-low heat. Add sage and garlic and cook for about 1–2 minutes.

4 Toss noodles with chicken and garlic and sage oil. Season with salt and pepper as desired.

Don't Have a Slow Cooker?
Slow-cooking the chicken gives it a softer and more crumbly texture, but if you don't have a slow cooker, you can bake the chicken ahead of time and just shred it with your fingers. It won't be as soft, but the texture will be similar.

Jerk-Inspired Chicken with Plantain Rice

Native to Jamaica, jerk chicken is marinated in a spice-filled marinade filled with sweet and spicy flavors. This recipe uses the most accessible jerk chicken spices, so you can conveniently reach into your spice cabinet at any time to make this meal. The plantain rice is also served Jamaican style, cooked with allspice, thyme, and coconut milk. For the chicken to have a strong flavor, be sure to marinate it overnight, although if you are short on time, 4 hours will do.

Serves 4

Ingredients for Jerk Chicken

- 4 free-range boneless, skinless chicken breasts
- ¼ cup malt vinegar
- 1½ tablespoons soy sauce
- 1 tablespoon thyme
- 2 teaspoons allspice
- 1 teaspoon cinnamon
- 1 teaspoon nutmeg
- 4 cloves garlic, minced
- ½ tablespoon minced ginger

Ingredients for Plantain Rice

- 4 large plantains
- 1 tablespoon extra-virgin olive oil
- 2 teaspoons garlic powder
- 1 teaspoon allspice
- 1 teaspoon thyme
- 1 teaspoon cumin
- Salt
- Pepper
- 1 cup unsweetened coconut milk

1. Place chicken breasts flat on a baking sheet. In a medium-sized bowl, mix together malt vinegar, soy sauce, thyme, allspice, cinnamon, nutmeg, garlic, and ginger. Pour over chicken breasts and refrigerate at a minimum 4 hours and for best results overnight.

2. Once chicken has marinated, preheat oven to 350°F. Bake for 30 minutes.

3. While chicken is baking, prepare Plantain Rice. Peel plantains, slice in half crosswise, and cut off both ends. Spiralize using a small-noodle blade. Convert plantain into bite-sized rice pieces by either cutting noodles with a knife or blending noodles in a food processor by pulsing until they form rice-like bits. You can also skip this step and mash the plantain into rice using a spatula once it's in the pan, which also works well.

4. Heat 1 tablespoon olive oil in a large pan on medium-low. Add plantains, breaking up into rice-sized bits with a spatula if you haven't already. Add garlic powder, allspice, thyme, cumin, and a dash of salt and pepper and cook for about 2–3 minutes. Add coconut milk and cook for about 4–5 minutes until coconut milk is absorbed. Serve chicken over rice.

Kale and Sun-Dried Tomato Sweet Potato Pasta Bake with Chicken

Creamy pasta bakes are quick and quite tasty, and the same goes for this one, except it's lightened up by using Greek yogurt and sun-dried tomato oil. This dish is lightly sauced, but if you prefer the bake to be more covered and saucy, double the amount of Greek yogurt and sun-dried tomatoes you use. I would purchase jarred sun-dried tomatoes with oil, as the oil is flavorful and adds to the sauce.

Serves 4

2 large sweet potatoes

1 medium onion

2 cloves garlic

2 free-range boneless, skinless chicken breasts

1½ tablespoons extra-virgin olive oil

2 cups kale leaves

½ cup Greek yogurt

½ cup sun-dried tomatoes

3 tablespoons sun-dried tomato oil

1 Preheat oven to 350°F. Cut sweet potatoes in half crosswise and slice off both ends. Spiralize using a small-noodle blade. Set aside. Chop onion and garlic. Slice chicken breasts into thin, ½"-wide strips.

2 In a large pan, heat olive oil on medium heat. Add garlic and onions and cook for about 2 minutes. Add chicken strips and cook for 2 minutes or so on each side. Add kale and mix it in for about 1 minute. Kale won't be fully cooked, but it should just be mixed with the chicken and onions.

3 In a separate large oven-safe pan or cast-iron skillet, add half of the spiralized noodles. Top with kale and chicken mixture. Press flat and cover with remaining noodles.

4 In a small bowl, combine Greek yogurt, sun-dried tomatoes, and sun-dried tomato oil. Mix until Greek yogurt and oil are smoothly combined. Pour over sweet potato dish, spreading evenly.

5 Bake for 15 minutes and then remove. Mix ingredients together, trying to evenly distribute everything, including sauce. The sweet potato and kale should have shrunk down, so it will be easier to stir together. Return to the oven and bake for an additional 20 minutes. Serve warm.

Honey Lemon Chicken Butternut Squash Pasta

Honey lemon pasta sounds like it would be a heavy and decadent dish, but when you use butternut squash noodles and a simple and light marinade, you're actually in for a healthy treat. This dish is filled with disease-fighting nutrients, whether it's the antioxidants in the butternut squash, the vitamin C in the lemon, or the antibacterial properties of honey. Make sure you marinate the chicken 30 minutes to an hour before you want to start cooking to maximize its flavor, but if you are short on time, even 10–15 minutes will work.

Serves 2

½ pound free-range boneless, skinless chicken breasts

2 tablespoons wild raw honey

2 tablespoons lemon juice

½ teaspoon thyme

½ teaspoon garlic powder

½ teaspoon cumin

1 large butternut squash

1 tablespoon extra-virgin olive oil

1 Slice chicken breasts into strips and then cut the strips in half. Lay the strips flat in a baking dish. In a small bowl, combine honey, lemon juice, thyme, garlic powder, and cumin until evenly blended. Reserve 2 tablespoons. Pour remaining mixture over the chicken breasts. Cover and refrigerate for 30–60 minutes.

2 Preheat oven to 425°F. Cut the bulbous end off your butternut squash and set aside. You will only be using the longer end to spiralize. Peel butternut squash until the top, tough surface is completely removed; then slice in half crosswise and cut off both ends. Spiralize using a small-noodle blade. Place noodles on an aluminum-foil-lined baking sheet and drizzle with olive oil. Roast noodles for 10–12 minutes.

3 When squash is finished, remove from oven and lower temperature to 350°F. Place chicken in the oven and bake for 30 minutes. Add chicken to noodles, tossing with the reserved marinade. Top with extra thyme if desired. Serve warm.

CHAPTER NINE
Fish and Seafood

Zucchini Shrimp Scampi

Shrimp scampi is simply shrimp tossed in butter, oil, and herbs, and it's often served with spaghetti. This scampi retains all the flavor of the shrimp while pairing it with zucchini noodles for a lightened-up but still rich and buttery flavor. Using ghee instead of regular butter removes the milk solids, making it friendlier for people with sensitive stomachs. It also has a higher smoke point, which is good for cooking the garlic and shrimp. This scampi has a little bit of a kick from the red chili flakes, so remove those if you don't want your dish to have any spice.

Serves 2

- 3 large zucchini
- 3 tablespoons extra-virgin olive oil, divided
- 2 tablespoons ghee (clarified butter)
- 2 tablespoons chopped garlic (about 6 cloves)
- 8 jumbo shrimp
- ½ cup finely chopped onion
- ¼ cup chopped fresh parsley
- 10 cherry tomatoes
- Juice of 2 small lemons
- ¼ teaspoon red chili flakes
- ¼ teaspoon salt
- ½ teaspoon pepper

1. Cut zucchini in half crosswise and slice off both ends. Spiralize using a small-noodle blade. Pat between two pieces of paper towel to remove excess moisture. Set aside.

2. In a large pan, heat 2 tablespoons olive oil and ghee on low heat. Add garlic and cook for 1 minute.

3. Turn heat to medium-low. Add shrimp and onion and cook for 5–6 minutes, stirring every minute or so.

4. While the shrimp are cooking, heat 1 tablespoon olive oil in a separate large pan on medium-low heat. Add zucchini and toss around for about 3 minutes. You want the zucchini to be undercooked, as it will cook down more when combined with sauce.

5. When shrimp are done, remove from heat. Then add parsley, tomatoes, lemon juice, and red chili flakes, stirring until everything is mixed evenly. Pour mixture over zucchini noodles and toss until evenly coated. Top with salt and pepper and serve warm.

California Roll in a Bowl

If you're a big fan of sushi, you're going to love this deconstructed California roll bowl. The traditional California roll is a combination of crab, avocado, and cucumber, and using quinoa instead of rice gives this bowl a healthier taste. You can choose to use real crab or imitation crab in this dish.

Serves 2

1 large cucumber
2 cups cooked quinoa
2 tablespoons sesame oil
5 tablespoons rice vinegar
1 cup crab/imitation crab
½ avocado
2 stalks green onion
1 tablespoon hemp seeds
1 tablespoon soy sauce

1 Cut cucumber in half crosswise and slice off both ends. Spiralize using a small-noodle blade. Place noodles between two paper towels to soak up extra moisture.

2 In a medium bowl, mix quinoa with sesame oil and rice vinegar. Split quinoa into two small bowls and top with cucumber noodles.

3 Chop crab/imitation crab into bite-sized pieces and place on top of quinoa and cucumber. Slice avocado into cubes and add to crab and quinoa bowl.

4 Finely chop green onion stalks. Top the bowls with green onion, hemp seeds, and soy sauce and serve immediately.

Zucchini Tuna Casserole

Casseroles are an ideal dish to make for large groups on a budget, but they can get unhealthy quickly. This tuna casserole uses zucchini noodles instead of egg noodles, and the zucchini works well in this dish because the texture greatly resembles regular noodles. This is a quick-prep dish that is flavorful, filling, and healthy, and it also won't break the bank. You can use any can of tuna, but opting for lighter versions will help you cut down on mercury consumption (though it contains slightly lower levels of omega-3 fatty acids). Either white or light will work here.

Serves 4–6

- 1 medium onion
- 3 medium zucchini
- 1 tablespoon extra-virgin olive oil
- ½ cup peas
- 2 (5-ounce) cans tuna
- ½ cup vegetable or chicken broth
- 1 tablespoon whole-wheat flour
- 1 cup mozzarella cheese

1 Preheat oven to 350°F. Dice onion. Cut zucchini in half crosswise, and slice off both ends. Spiralize using a straight-noodle blade so the noodles come out in waves.

2 Heat olive oil in a large pan on medium heat. Add onions and cook for 5 minutes. Add zucchini and cook for another 2–3 minutes. Add peas, tuna, vegetable broth, and flour and stir until ingredients are mixed evenly. Then add ½ cup mozzarella cheese and mix in.

3 Transfer to a 10″ × 6″ casserole dish and sprinkle remaining mozzarella cheese over the top. Bake for 30 minutes. Let slightly cool and serve warm.

Asian-Inspired Sweet Potato Noodles with Salmon

Salmon is always a good go-to when it comes to fish, and it's often prepared simply, dressed with lemon or other vegetables. But salmon doesn't have to be plain, and it can be incorporated into many types of cuisine. This Asian-inspired salmon is topped with a sauce that tastes similar to teriyaki, and the noodles are cooked in sesame oil, giving them an Eastern flair.

Serves 2

1 wild-caught salmon fillet
5 cloves garlic
1 tablespoon extra-virgin olive oil
2 large sweet potatoes
1 tablespoon sesame oil

Ingredients for Sauce

2 tablespoons sesame oil
2 cloves garlic, finely chopped
2 teaspoons grated ginger
4 tablespoons soy sauce
2 teaspoons coconut sugar
2 stalks green onion, chopped

1 Preheat oven to 350°F. Spread salmon on an aluminum-foil-lined baking sheet. Finely chop garlic and spread on top of salmon. Top with olive oil and bake for about 20 minutes or until salmon is flaky and no longer pink.

2 Peel sweet potatoes, cut in half crosswise, and slice off both ends. Spiralize using a small-noodle blade.

3 Heat 1 tablespoon sesame oil in a large pan on medium heat. Add sweet potatoes, cover, and cook for about 9 minutes or until sweet potatoes are soft.

4 While sweet potatoes are cooking, prepare the sauce. In a small saucepan, heat 2 tablespoons sesame oil, garlic, ginger, soy sauce, and coconut sugar, stirring frequently until it comes to a boil. Remove from heat and mix in green onion.

5 When sweet potatoes are ready, add to a plate or bowl, top with salmon, and drizzle sauce over dish until fish and noodles are covered. Serve warm.

White Wine Scallops over Golden Beets

Aside from its delicious and rich wine-flavored sauce, this recipe is great because you get to use the entire beet plant. Many people buy beets and toss the greens, but these leaves are extremely flavorful and edible, and they should be incorporated into cooking. Beet greens are extremely high in iron, calcium, and magnesium, and they have a mild, sweet flavor similar to spinach.

Serves 2

- 6 golden beets
- 3 tablespoons extra-virgin olive oil, divided
- 2 tablespoons minced shallots
- 2 cups chopped beet greens
- ¾ cup white wine
- 6 jumbo scallops
- ½ tablespoon ghee (clarified butter)

1 Preheat oven to 425°F. Peel beets and cut off both ends. Spiralize using a small-noodle blade. Place noodles on an aluminum-foil-lined baking sheet and drizzle with 1 table-spoon olive oil. Bake for 15–20 minutes.

2 In a large, pan, heat 2 tablespoons olive oil on medium heat. Add shallots and cook for 1 minute. Then add beet greens and cook for an additional 3 minutes.

3 Pour in wine and bring to a boil. Add scallops and ghee, and reduce to a simmer. Cook for about 3 minutes on each side. When beet noodles are finished cooking, top them with scallops and wine sauce and serve warm.

Zucchini Spaghetti con le Sarde

Pasta con le sarde is a traditional Sicilian dish prepared with sardines and anchovies. This Sicilian staple is commonly cooked with bucatini, a thick spaghetti, but zucchini makes a wonderful substitute. If you want your zucchini to look more like bucatini, peel before you spiralize. Just be sure you don't cook down your zucchini too much before adding the sauce; it will soften from the heat of the sardine sauce.

Serves 2

- 2 large zucchini
- ¼ teaspoon salt
- ½ head fennel (including leaves)
- ½ medium onion
- 5 tablespoons extra-virgin olive oil, divided
- ¼ cup pine nuts
- 4 sardines
- 2 anchovy fillets
- ¼ cup currants
- 2 tablespoons bread crumbs

Zucchini-to-Sauce Ratio
This recipe yields a pasta heavy in the sauce, but if you prefer your noodles to be lightly tossed in the sardine sauce, then consider adding more zucchini noodles to dilute the impact of the sardines. One or two more zucchini should do the trick.

1 Cut zucchini in half crosswise; slice off both ends. Spiralize using a small-noodle blade. Set aside.

2 Fill a medium-sized pot with water, add salt, and bring to a boil. Add fennel and boil for 10–15 minutes. Remove fennel from water and chop fennel fronds (the leaves); set them aside for later. Keep 1–2 cups of fennel water for the sauce.

3 Finely chop the onion. In a large pan, heat 2 tablespoons olive oil on medium heat. Add onions and cook for about 3–4 minutes until onions are translucent. Then add ½ cup reserved fennel water, fennel fronds, and pine nuts; simmer for 4–5 minutes.

4 While onions and pine nuts are cooking, finely chop sardines and anchovies. Heat 1 tablespoon olive oil in a medium-sized pan on medium-low heat, add the fish, and cook for about 2–3 minutes.

5 Add sardines and anchovies to the pan with onion. Add ¼ cup reserved fennel water and currants to the pan, stir the sauce, and simmer for 2–3 minutes.

6 In a small pan, heat 1 tablespoon olive oil on medium heat to toast bread crumbs. Add bread crumbs and stir constantly for about 3–4 minutes until they are golden brown. After sardine sauce has simmered, add bread crumbs. Remove sauce from heat.

7 Heat 1 tablespoon olive oil in a large pan on medium heat. Add zucchini and cook for about 2 minutes or until just slightly softened. Remove from heat and add sardine sauce, tossing until evenly coated. Serve warm.

Rainbow Carrot Noodles with Ahi Poke

This is a quick-make ahi bowl that takes the Hawaiian preparation of cubed ahi and serves it over a bed of multicolored carrot noodles. It is simply dressed with sesame oil and lemon, making it a light and refreshing bowl. These carrot noodles are just slightly roasted, making them a little bit softer while keeping them just firm enough and crunchy to hold the weight of the ahi tuna. If you prefer, you can cook the noodles for longer to make them softer, or don't cook them at all if you like them raw.

Serves 2

3 large carrots (yellow, orange, and purple)
1 tablespoon olive oil
½ pound sashimi-grade wild-caught ahi tuna
1 teaspoon sesame oil
1 stalk green onion
½ teaspoon sesame seeds
1 lemon
Soy sauce (to serve on side)

1 Preheat oven to 400°F. Cut off both ends of carrots and slice in half crosswise. Spiralize using a small-noodle blade. Toss noodles together in a medium bowl with 1 tablespoon olive oil, mixing the different-colored noodles together. Place on an aluminum-foil-lined baking sheet and roast for 4 minutes. Remove from oven and place in a medium bowl.

2 Slice ahi tuna into 1" (or slightly smaller) cubes. Add fish to a small bowl and combine with sesame oil and green onions until evenly coated.

3 Top carrot noodles with tuna and sprinkle with sesame seeds. Squeeze lemon over and serve immediately with a side of soy sauce.

Choosing Your Ahi

The key to a good bowl of poke is using fresh fish. Buy it from a reputable source, such as your local fish market, and be sure it is sashimi grade, so you're safe to eat it raw. Look for pieces that are bright in color and don't have too many white lines.

Parsnip Pasta with "Creamy" Crab Vodka Sauce

One of my favorite pasta dishes when I was younger was penne à la vodka. I couldn't quite understand how the vodka made the pink sauce that much better, but somehow it did (and still does). This vodka sauce is lightened up by replacing cream with cashews and almond milk, which makes this dish a good option for people who are dairy-free or who follow the Paleo Diet. Add a bit of crab and you have an even richer sauce that goes well with the subtle and soft flavors of the parsnip.

Serves 4

3 or 4 large parsnips

2 tablespoons extra-virgin olive oil

Ingredients for Crab Vodka Sauce

1 medium onion

4 cloves garlic

2 tablespoons extra-virgin olive oil

1 (28-ounce) can crushed tomatoes

½ cup vodka

¾ cup raw cashews

1 cup unsweetened almond milk

½ cup crab leg meat

1 Peel parsnips and cut in half crosswise. Chop off ends and spiralize using a small-noodle blade. In a large pan, heat 2 tablespoons olive oil on medium heat. Add parsnips and mix around so they're evenly coated with olive oil. Cover and cook for 6–8 minutes until parsnips are soft, stirring every 2 minutes or so. Turn off heat and set aside.

2 Finely chop onion and garlic. In a large pan or pot, heat 2 tablespoons olive oil on medium heat. Add onion and garlic and cook for about 4 minutes. Add crushed tomatoes and vodka and bring to a boil. Then reduce heat to medium-low and cook for about 7 minutes or until the alcohol cooks off.

3 While tomato mixture is simmering, create your "cream." Add cashews and almond milk to a blender or food processor and blend until smooth. After tomato mixture is done, add cream and crab, mixing evenly. Cook for about 1–2 minutes on low. Serve over parsnip noodles.

Coconut Curry Shrimp Zucchini Noodles

Seafood dishes can sometimes be overpowering, but when you mix in the strong flavors of coconut and curry, it helps to mask that salty, fishy taste that some people don't enjoy. This dish comes from Thailand, where coconut is a frequent ingredient. This fragrant and filling dish is dairy-free, and it's loaded with spices that not only create a satisfying sauce but can help boost your immune system and help keep your body on track.

Serves 2

- 3 tablespoons extra-virgin olive oil, divided
- 2 cloves garlic, chopped
- 1" piece of ginger, grated
- Zest of 1 lemon
- 1 tablespoon soy sauce
- 1 tablespoon curry powder
- 1 cup coconut milk
- 8–10 medium shrimp
- 3 medium zucchini
- 1½ tablespoons coconut oil, divided
- 3 stalks green onion
- Red chili flakes

1 Begin by preparing sauce. In a small saucepan, heat 2 tablespoons olive oil on medium-low heat. Add garlic, ginger, lemon zest, and soy sauce and cook for about 2 minutes or until it begins to bubble and get fragrant. Mix in curry powder, then add coconut milk. Stir together, bring to a boil, and cook for about 1–2 minutes to thicken, stirring occasionally. Remove from heat and set aside.

2 In a large pan, heat 1 tablespoon olive oil on medium heat. Add shrimp and cook for 4–5 minutes or until shrimp turn pink and opaque. Set shrimp aside.

3 Cut zucchini in half crosswise and slice off both ends. Spiralize using a small-noodle blade. Pat zucchini noodles with a paper towel to remove excess moisture. In the same large pan, heat 1 tablespoon coconut oil on medium-low heat. Add zucchini noodles and cook for 3–4 minutes or until zucchini begins to get soft. Remove from pan and set aside.

4 Cut 2 of the green onion stalks into large pieces and finely chop the remaining stalk. Save the finely chopped green onion for garnish. Heat ½ tablespoon coconut oil in the pan on medium heat. Add the large green onion pieces and cook for about 2–3 minutes or until green onion softens.

5 Lower heat and add zucchini noodles, shrimp, and coconut sauce; mix together until noodles are evenly coated. Serve warm and top with remaining green onion and red chili flakes to taste.

Tilapia with Potato Noodles and Lemon Chili Pesto

Tilapia is a mild, white fish that goes with many types of cooking, and it's a good choice for people looking for a less "fishy" taste. The strong flavor in this dish comes from the lemon chili pesto, which provides a spicy kick to an otherwise plain plate. If you don't want your pesto to be as spicy, you can prepare it more like a traditional pesto, and cut the amount of chili flakes in half or nix them altogether. When buying your fish, look for tilapia sourced from the United States, as it is the most environmentally friendly as well as nutritious option.

Serves 2

¾ pound U.S.-bred tilapia

3½ tablespoons extra-virgin olive oil, divided

Juice of ½ lemon

1 large russet potato

¼ teaspoon salt

¼ teaspoon pepper

2 tablespoons pine nuts

½ cup basil

Juice of 2 lemons

1 tablespoon red chili flakes

5 cherry tomatoes, halved

1 Preheat oven to 450°F. Place tilapia fillets on a baking sheet lined with aluminum foil. Drizzle ½ tablespoon olive oil and lemon juice over fish and place in the oven. Bake for about 8 minutes or until tilapia is flaky.

2 While tilapia is baking, spiralize potato. Peel potato, cut in half crosswise, and slice off both ends. Spiralize using a small-noodle blade.

3 In a medium pan, heat 1 tablespoon olive oil on medium heat. Add potato noodles and lightly stir them into the oil; season with salt and pepper. Cover and cook for about 8–10 minutes until noodles are soft.

4 Prepare pesto by adding pine nuts, basil, lemon juice, and 1 tablespoon olive oil to a blender or food processor and blend until almost smooth. Add another 1 tablespoon olive oil and the red chili flakes and blend for just a few seconds to evenly disperse chili flakes.

5 Serve tilapia and tomatoes over potato noodles and drizzle pesto over entire dish. Serve warm.

White Sweet Potato Noodles with Smoked Salmon and Asparagus

Asparagus and salmon are often paired together for breakfast meals, but there's no reason they can't be made in a lunch or dinner entrée. This pasta is savory with slightly sweet hints from the white sweet potato and lemon, but it's a light entrée that contains a little kick. Using smoked salmon gives this dish a more unique flavor, but if you want to use regular salmon instead, that would work as well. Just bake and add to the dish when you would the smoked salmon.

Serves 2

24 mini asparagus spears (½ bunch)

2 tablespoons extra-virgin olive oil, divided

1 large white sweet potato

2 cloves garlic, chopped

4 ounces smoked salmon

Juice of 1 lemon

¼ cup grated Parmesan cheese

1 Preheat oven to 425°F. Chop off the bottom ½" of the asparagus stalks. Spread asparagus on an aluminum-foil-lined baking sheet and drizzle 1 tablespoon olive oil over spears. Bake for 15 minutes. Remove from oven and chop; set aside.

2 Peel sweet potato, cut in half crosswise, and slice off both ends. Spiralize using a small-noodle blade. Heat 1 tablespoon olive oil in a large pan on medium heat and add garlic; cook for 1 minute. Add noodles, cover, and cook for about 6 minutes or until noodles are soft.

3 Turn heat to low and add asparagus, smoked salmon, and lemon juice, tossing around until ingredients are evenly mixed. Top with Parmesan cheese and serve warm or cold.

Plantain Rice Paella

Paella is one of the most famous dishes of Spain. It's a beautiful combination of seafood, rice, and saffron, and it is usually served straight out of the frying pan, known as the paellera. For this version of the national Spanish dish, plantain rice is used instead of white rice. This particular paella uses shrimp and mussels, but oftentimes clams, scallops, or squid are used as well.

Serves 4

- 3 green plantains
- 1 large onion
- 6 cloves garlic
- ¾ cup cherry tomatoes
- ½ red bell pepper
- 2 tablespoons extra-virgin olive oil
- 2 cups chicken broth
- 1 teaspoon paprika
- 2 pinches saffron
- 6 jumbo shrimp
- 12 mussels
- Bunch of parsley

1 Remove peel from plantains, slice in half, and chop off both ends. If your plantains are very ripe, the peel may be hard to remove, but you can use a knife to help remove it. Spiralize using a small-noodle blade.

2 Chop onion, garlic, cherry tomatoes, and red bell pepper. Heat 2 tablespoons olive oil on medium heat. Add onions and garlic and cook for 5 minutes. Lower heat to medium-low and add plantains. Cook for 2 minutes, and while plantains are cooking use a spatula to break up the plantains into smaller, rice-sized pieces (you can also pulse in a food processor prior to cooking or chop using a knife).

3 Add a cup of broth along with paprika and saffron, and cook for 5 minutes. Then add another cup of broth along with tomatoes, pepper, shrimp, and mussels. Bring to medium heat and cook for an additional 5 minutes. Top with fresh parsley and serve warm.

Cook Time Warning
Because plantains are used instead of rice, you have to be careful how long you simmer the paella. If the plantain rice sits in too much broth for too long, it will turn an unattractive brown color, although the taste will only be slightly affected.

Mahi Mahi over Zucchini Noodles with Mango Salsa

Named by the Hawaiians, mahi mahi is a tropical fish with a delicate and mild flavor. It is enjoyed often in tropical climates, so it's only fitting it be topped with something like a mango salsa. When buying mahi mahi, look for a variety caught in the Atlantic off the coast of the United States, which is the best for the environment.

Serves 1 or 2

1 medium mahi mahi fillet
2 medium zucchini
1 tablespoon coconut oil

Ingredients for Mango Salsa

1 cup chopped mango
⅓ cup chopped red onion
1 cup chopped tomatoes
¼ jalapeño, chopped
Juice of 2 limes
Dash of salt

1 Broil mahi mahi for 6 minutes on each side.

2 While fish is cooking, cut zucchini in half crosswise and slice off both ends. Spiralize using a small-noodle blade. In a large pan, heat coconut oil on medium heat. Add zucchini and cook for about 5 minutes or until noodles are soft.

3 To make salsa, combine chopped mango, red onion, tomatoes, and jalapeño. Toss with lime juice and a dash of salt.

4 Place noodles on a plate and top with fish and salsa. Serve warm or chilled.

Golden Beet Linguine and Clams

The only times I have ever enjoyed linguine and clam pasta were when eating out at restaurants; it seemed complicated to make on your own. Turns out, it's really not. You can find clams at your local seafood market, or even frozen at the grocery store, and both work well. Golden beet noodles replace linguine, and since they are sturdy with a slightly sweet flavor, they go well with the seafood-heavy sauce.

Serves 2

- 3 medium golden beets
- 2 tablespoons extra-virgin olive oil, divided
- ½ pound fresh or frozen clams
- ½ medium onion
- 4 cloves garlic
- ¼ cup white wine
- ¼ cup clam juice
- 1 tablespoon finely chopped parsley
- 1 teaspoon red chili flakes

1 Preheat oven to 425°F. Peel beets and slice off both ends. Spiralize using a small-noodle blade. Spread beets evenly on an aluminum-foil-lined baking sheet and drizzle with 1 tablespoon olive oil. Bake for 15 minutes.

2 Bring a medium pot of water to boil. Add clams and boil for about 10 minutes or until clams begin to open. Set aside the clams in their shell.

3 Finely chop onion and garlic. In a large pan, heat 1 tablespoon olive oil on medium heat. Add onions and garlic and cook for 3–4 minutes. Add white wine, clam juice, and reserved whole clams back in and simmer for 4–5 minutes.

4 Top beet noodles with clam sauce and clams and sprinkle with parsley and red chili flakes. Serve warm.

Garlicky-Fried Oysters with Parsnip Noodles

Although raw oysters are quite delicious, there's another cheaper and easier way to enjoy them: from the can. They take on an even richer flavor when lightly fried, and mixed with the parsnip noodles, they make for an easy seafood dish that's inexpensive and simple to prepare. Canned oysters are typically found at any grocery store, and they are a good supplement to entrées, as they're filled with zinc, iron, vitamin B_{12}, and vitamin A.

Serves 2

1 large parsnip
3 tablespoons extra-virgin
   olive oil, divided
4 cloves garlic
1 (3-ounce) can oysters
1 tablespoon whole-wheat
   flour
1 cup arugula
Juice of 1 lemon
1 tablespoon flaxseed meal
¼ teaspoon pepper

1 Peel parsnip, cut in half, and slice off both ends. Spiralize using a small-noodle blade. Heat 1 tablespoon olive oil in a large pan on medium heat. Add parsnips, cover, and cook for 8–10 minutes. Remove parsnips from pan and set aside.

2 Finely chop garlic. Heat 2 tablespoons olive oil on medium heat. Add garlic and cook for 1 minute. Dip oysters into whole-wheat flour and cook for 2 minutes on each side.

3 Lower heat and add back in parsnips along with arugula and toss. Remove from heat and toss noodles in lemon juice, flaxseed meal, and pepper. Serve warm.

Lemon Saffron Cod over Butternut Squash Noodles

Cod, like salmon, is another heart-healthy fish filled with omega-3 fatty acids. Its mild flavor makes it a versatile fish, and in this pasta dish it's dressed up with a rich, buttery saffron sauce that brings the cod and squash together. When choosing cod, it's best to choose Pacific cod over Atlantic cod. Pacific cod is more environmentally friendly and it has a softer and more delicate texture, making it a good option to be served over noodles.

Serves 2

1 large butternut squash
2½ tablespoons extra-virgin olive oil, divided
1 cup halved cherry tomatoes
2 medium cod fillets
½ lemon

Ingredients for Lemon Saffron Sauce

2 tablespoons ghee (clarified butter)
2 tablespoons chopped garlic
1 generous pinch of saffron
1 tablespoon lemon juice
1 tablespoon white wine

1 Preheat oven to 425°F. Cut the bulbous end off your butternut squash and set aside. You will only be using the longer end to spiralize. Peel butternut squash until the top, tough surface is completely removed; then slice in half crosswise and cut off both ends. Spiralize using a small-noodle blade. Place noodles on an aluminum-foil-lined baking sheet and drizzle with 1 tablespoon olive oil. Roast noodles for 10–12 minutes.

2 Place cherry tomatoes on an aluminum-foil-lined baking sheet and drizzle with 1 tablespoon olive oil. Roast for 20–25 minutes or until tomatoes have become soft.

3 Lower oven temperature to 400°F. Place cod fillets on a baking sheet and drizzle with ½ tablespoon olive oil and a squeeze of lemon. Bake for about 15 minutes or until fish is flaky.

4 While cod is baking, heat ghee in a small pan or pot on low heat. Add garlic to pan and cook for 1 minute. Add saffron and stir. Add lemon juice and white wine and raise the temperature to medium. Cook for 2–3 minutes.

5 When cod is finished, top squash noodles with roasted tomatoes and cod. Pour sauce over entire dish and serve warm.

Pineapple Plantain "Fried Rice" with Shrimp

You can make your own, lighter fried rice at home using anything from brown rice to quinoa and even spiralized plantains. Since plantains are starchy and make such a great rice substitution, they make the perfect fried rice ingredient.

Serves 2

- 2 green plantains
- 4 cloves garlic, divided
- 2 tablespoons extra-virgin olive oil, divided
- ⅓ cup vegetable broth
- Salt
- Pepper
- 8–10 medium shrimp (about ½ pound)
- ½ medium onion
- ½ tablespoon coconut oil
- ⅓ cup chopped pineapple
- ¼ cup shredded coconut
- 2 large cage-free eggs
- 1 tablespoon chopped cilantro

1 Peel plantains, cut in half, and slice off both ends. Spiralize using a small-noodle blade. You can choose to put noodles in a food processor and pulse into rice, chop with a knife, or put noodles into the pan and break pieces up using a spatula.

2 Chop 2 cloves garlic. Heat 1 tablespoon olive oil in a large pan on medium heat. Add garlic to pan and cook for 1–2 minutes. Add plantains, breaking into small pieces of rice if you haven't already. Cook for 2 minutes, then add vegetable broth. Cook for 2–3 minutes and then season with salt and pepper. Set rice aside.

3 Heat 1 tablespoon olive oil on medium heat. Add shrimp and cook for 4–5 minutes or until shrimp turn pink and opaque. Set shrimp aside.

4 Chop onion and remaining 2 cloves garlic. Heat coconut oil in the pan on medium heat. Sauté chopped onion, remaining garlic, and pineapple until onions are translucent and slightly browned on the outside (think of a grilled effect), about 4–5 minutes.

5 Once onions and pineapple are cooked, mix in plantain rice, shrimp, and shredded coconut. Turn heat to medium-high and crack eggs into the pan. Let sit for 1 minute and then use a spatula to mix in to the plantains. To get the fried rice effect, you want the egg to be somewhat chunky in your dish, without mixing together too much the yolk and the whites. Cook for about 1–2 minutes or until eggs are fully cooked.

6 Remove from heat and mix in cilantro. Serve warm.

CHAPTER TEN
Side Dishes

Garlic Parsley Curly Fries with Sriracha Yogurt Dipping Sauce

One of the best aspects of the spiralizer is that it can turn otherwise unhealthy meals into lighter and healthier versions. These French fries are a perfect example of how you can make a typical fast food without the deep-frying or excess sodium. These curly potatoes are baked to crispy perfection, and you can enjoy them with an easy two-step, low-fat dipping sauce—just be prepared to handle the heat!

Serves 2

- 2 large russet potatoes
- 3 tablespoons extra-virgin olive oil or vegetable oil
- 4 cloves garlic, finely chopped
- ¼ cup finely chopped parsley
- ½ cup Greek yogurt
- 1 tablespoon sriracha

1 Preheat oven to 450°F. Cut potatoes in half crosswise and slice off both ends. Spiralize using a large-noodle blade and put noodles into a large bowl.

2 Add olive oil, garlic, and parsley to potato bowl and toss until evenly coated. Place on a baking sheet lined with aluminum foil and bake for 15–20 minutes or until fries are crispy.

3 To make dipping sauce, just combine Greek yogurt and sriracha in a small bowl and mix until blended.

Apple Coleslaw

This healthy version of coleslaw uses spiralized cabbage as well as spiralized apple. It's tossed in a dairy-free honey mustard dressing, making it a healthier option with a sweet and tangy kick. It can be served as a side salad, on a sandwich or burger, or with chicken. You can refrigerate the slaw before serving, which will allow the flavors to marinate, though it's not necessary. If you don't have Dijon mustard, you can also use regular yellow mustard, although the dressing will be more mild and a little more sweet.

Serves 4

- 1 head green cabbage
- 2 apples
- 3 tablespoons chopped chives
- 2 tablespoons chopped cilantro
- 4 tablespoons Dijon mustard
- 4 tablespoons wild raw honey
- 2 tablespoons extra-virgin olive oil
- 2 tablespoons white wine vinegar
- ¼ teaspoon pepper
- ¼ teaspoon salt

1 Cut off the end of the cabbage and peel off outer layer. Spiralize using a straight-noodle blade and put spiralized cabbage into a large bowl.

2 Spiralize apples using a small-noodle blade and add to the bowl with cabbage. Add chopped chives and cilantro and toss.

3 To make dressing, mix together mustard, honey, olive oil, and vinegar in a small bowl until everything is combined evenly. Pour over cabbage bowl and toss until salad is coated evenly. Top with salt and pepper. Serve immediately or refrigerate to chill.

Butternut Squash "Mac and Cheese"

If you're a fan of Kraft macaroni and cheese, you'll be sure to love this healthy, lightened-up substitute. Free of chemicals and refined flour, this version of macaroni and cheese uses spiralized squash as pasta noodles and two types of cheese, along with Greek yogurt for extra creaminess. You can get creative with any type of cheese you like, but this recipe calls for Cheddar like the classic comfort dish. Your kids will have no idea they aren't eating the real deal, as the physical resemblance is pretty uncanny.

Serves 4

- 1 large butternut squash
- 2 tablespoons extra-virgin olive oil
- 2 cloves garlic, finely chopped
- ⅓ cup grated Parmesan cheese
- ⅓ cup grated sharp Cheddar cheese
- 3 tablespoons Greek yogurt

1 Cut the bulbous end off your butternut squash and set aside. You will be using the longer end to spiralize. Peel butternut squash until the top, tough surface is completely removed; then slice in half crosswise and cut off both ends. Spiralize using a small-noodle blade.

2 Heat olive oil in a large pan on medium heat. Add garlic and squash noodles and stir around the pan so that noodles are evenly coated with olive oil and garlic. Cover and cook for about 7 minutes or until noodles are super soft. Lower flame and with a spatula press onto the noodles to break them into smaller, bite-sized pieces.

3 Add Parmesan cheese, Cheddar cheese, and Greek yogurt and mix thoroughly on low heat until cheese is melted and noodles are evenly coated. Serve immediately while warm.

Beets with Mint Pistachio Pesto

You can't go wrong with noodles and pesto. They can, however, quickly get boring. A classic basil and pine nut pesto is delicious, but pestos are so versatile, why just stick to one herb or nut? A mint pesto is a great palate cleanser, and it will leave you feeling refreshed, especially blended with the creaminess of the pistachios. Since the beets are roasted, their sweet flavor is enhanced. Combine that with the savoriness of the Mediterranean-inspired pesto, and I can guarantee no one will be calling this noodle dish boring.

Serves 2

5 red beets

1½ tablespoons extra-virgin olive oil

Ingredients for Mint Pistachio Pesto

½ cup fresh mint

4 tablespoons pistachio meat

2 cloves garlic

Juice of 2 small lemons

4 tablespoons extra-virgin olive oil

1 Preheat oven to 425°F. Peel beets and cut off both ends. Spiralize using a small-noodle blade. Place noodles on an aluminum-foil-lined baking sheet and drizzle with 1½ tablespoons olive oil. Bake for 15 minutes or until soft but not shriveled.

2 While beets are roasting, prepare pesto. Add mint, pistachios, garlic, lemon juice, and olive oil to a blender or food processor and blend until smooth.

3 When beets are finished, toss noodles with pesto. Serve warm or chill.

Cajun-Spiced Jicama Shoestring Fries

When you think jicama, it's not typical to think of something hot like fries. But when you spiralize one of these, you get a completely different flavor than when served chilled. In fact, jicama is a great substitute for potato when it comes to French fries, and these root vegetables really soak up the Cajun spices, making them a flavorful and healthy alternative to indulgent comfort food.

Serves 4

2 large jicamas
1 tablespoon extra-virgin olive oil
2 teaspoons cayenne pepper
2 teaspoons oregano
2 teaspoons thyme
2 teaspoons paprika
1 teaspoon red chili flakes

1 Preheat oven to 400°F. Peel jicamas, slice in half, and cut off both ends. Spiralize using a small-noodle blade and place into a large bowl. Add olive oil and all remaining ingredients and toss until noodles are evenly coated.

2 Place jicama on an aluminum-foil-lined baking sheet, spreading evenly. Bake for 15 minutes, then flip fries using a spatula. Bake for another 10 minutes. Let cool for about 5–10 minutes and serve warm.

Use More Than You Think
These jicama fries shrink down a lot more than you would think, so if you're serving a larger group, opt for more jicama. These make a great side dish, but if you're making it the main focus, spiralize away!

Plantain-Rice Stuffed Red Bell Peppers

Peppers are a great source of antioxidants and nutrients, and turning them into a side dish by stuffing them is a fun way to switch up your vegetables. Stuffed peppers are often filled with white rice, but using plantains eliminates the need for refined carbs, and adds an extra, slightly sweet flavor that complements the pepper nicely. The key to this dish is the seasoned plantains, which carry the flavor of this bright and fun side dish. I used kale as a green, but this recipe also works with spinach, chard, or any other leafy green that can be wilted.

Makes 8 peppers

- 4 red bell peppers
- 4 tablespoons extra-virgin olive oil, divided
- 3 green plantains
- 1 medium onion
- 4 cloves garlic
- ½ teaspoon cumin
- ½ teaspoon pepper
- ¼ teaspoon salt
- ¼ cup vegetable broth
- 1 bunch kale (about 5 cups)
- 1 tablespoon white wine vinegar
- ¼ cup pine nuts
- 1 tablespoon finely chopped parsley
- Juice of 2 lemons
- ¼ cup water

1. Preheat oven to 400°F. Slice bell peppers in half lengthwise. Remove seeds and brush the outside and inside of the peppers using about 1 tablespoon olive oil. Place cut side down on a baking sheet and bake for 12–15 minutes until peppers begin to slightly soften. Remove from oven and flip peppers; let cool.

2. Peel plantains, cut in half, and slice off both ends. Spiralize using a small-noodle blade. Chop onions and garlic. Convert plantains into bite-sized rice pieces by either cutting noodles with a knife or pulsing noodles in a food processor until they form rice-like bits. You can also skip this step and convert the plantains into rice using a spatula once they're in the pan.

3. Heat 2 tablespoons olive oil in a large pan on medium heat. Add garlic and onions, and cook for 4–5 minutes. Add plantains and cook for 4–5 minutes. If you haven't already, break up noodles into rice using a spatula by pressing down onto noodles until they turn into rice-sized pieces.

4. Add cumin, pepper, salt, and broth and stir everything in evenly. Cook for about 1–2 minutes or until broth is dissolved. Remove from

heat and set aside.

5 Remove kale leaves from stem and finely chop leaves. Heat 1 tablespoon olive oil on medium heat. Add kale and white wine vinegar and cook for 3–4 minutes.

6 Mix in kale, pine nuts, parsley, and lemon juice with the plantains. Spoon mixture into red peppers and add peppers to a baking dish. Add ¼ cup water to baking dish and cover with aluminum foil. Cook for 10 minutes and then remove foil. Cook for an additional 5–7 minutes. Serve warm.

Spinach and Artichoke Potato Bake

What do you do when you like spinach and artichoke dip so much? Make it into a full-sized casserole! Just imagine a creamy potato casserole combined with the can't-go-wrong combination of spinach and artichoke, and you have this decadent spiralized bake. This may sound heavy and fattening, but this dish is lightened up by using mostly Greek yogurt instead of cream, with just a sprinkle of Parmesan cheese.

Serves 4–6

- 2 large russet potatoes
- 2½ tablespoons extra-virgin olive oil, divided
- ½ medium onion
- 4 cloves garlic
- 3 cups frozen spinach, defrosted
- 2 cups chopped artichoke hearts
- 1 cup Greek yogurt
- ½ cup grated Parmesan cheese
- 2 large cage-free eggs
- 1 tablespoon whole-wheat flour
- ¼ tablespoon salt
- ½ teaspoon pepper
- ⅛ cup bread crumbs

1 Preheat oven to 350°F. Peel potatoes, slice in half crosswise, and cut off both ends. Spiralize using a small- or large-noodle blade.

2 In a large pan, heat 1 tablespoon olive oil on medium heat. Add noodles, cover, and cook for about 10 minutes until potatoes are almost soft. Transfer to a large bowl.

3 Finely chop onions and garlic. Heat 1 tablespoon olive oil in the pan on medium-low heat. Add onions and garlic and cook for 2–3 minutes. Then add spinach and artichoke and cook for an additional 2–3 minutes. Remove from heat and let cool for 1–2 minutes before adding to bowl with potatoes.

4 In a medium bowl, combine Greek yogurt, cheese, eggs, flour, salt, and pepper and mix until ingredients are thoroughly combined. Add mixture to potato bowl and combine all ingredients.

5 Grease a 7" × 13" baking dish with ½ tablespoon olive oil. Spoon mixture into baking dish, spreading evenly. Sprinkle with bread crumbs and bake for 30–35 minutes. Let cool for 5–10 minutes and serve warm.

Savory Plantain Mushroom Risotto

Since plantains are so starchy and soft, they make an excellent substitute for risotto, and they don't take nearly as long to cook! You want to look for plantains that are not yet ripe for this dish, as they will be more savory. You can use any mushrooms of choice for the risotto, though white mushrooms work best. Experiment with a blend for more texture and heartiness.

Serves 4

3 large plantains

4 tablespoons extra-virgin olive oil, divided

4 cloves garlic

1 small onion

2 cups chopped mushrooms

2 cups chicken or vegetable broth

½ cup grated Parmesan cheese

¼ teaspoon salt

½ teaspoon pepper

1 Peel plantains and cut in half crosswise. Spiralize using a small-noodle blade.

2 Convert plantains into bite-sized rice pieces by either cutting noodles with a knife or pulsing noodles in a food processor until they form rice-like bits. You can also skip this step and mash the plantains into rice using a spatula once they're in the pan.

3 Chop garlic and onions. In a large pan, heat 2 tablespoons olive oil on medium-low heat. Add garlic, onions, and mushrooms and cook for about 3–4 minutes. Add plantain rice and cook for an additional 2–3 minutes. Add 1 cup chicken or vegetable broth and cook until broth is fully absorbed. Then add an additional 1 cup and cook until broth is absorbed again.

4 Once broth is fully absorbed, remove from heat and add Parmesan cheese, salt, pepper, and 2 tablespoons olive oil; mix until creamy. Serve warm.

Risotto Too Sweet?
Your rice shouldn't taste sweet, and if it does, your plantain might be a little bit too ripe. Look for one that is more green than yellow, and season with more olive oil, cheese, or salt and pepper to counteract any existing sweetness.

Turnip Noodles with Vegan Truffle Herb Cream Sauce

Think of these noodles as fettuccine Alfredo with a twist. Turnip noodles are sturdy and contain a bit of a kick, but paired with the rich creaminess of the herb sauce, they're a hearty and filling meat-free dish. Like most other cashew-based sauces, it's essential that you soak your cashews overnight for maximum creaminess. Feel free to experiment with other herbs beyond oregano and rosemary, and you can even opt for fresh herbs if you want a stronger flavor. If you don't have truffle salt, don't fret—the sauce is still quite tasty on its own.

Serves 2-4

2 large turnips
1 tablespoon extra-virgin olive oil
¼ teaspoon salt

Ingredients for Vegan Truffle Herb Cream Sauce

½ cup soaked cashews
2 tablespoons nutritional yeast
½ tablespoon garlic powder
½ tablespoon oregano
½ tablespoon rosemary
½ cup filtered water
½ teaspoon truffle salt

1 Preheat oven to 425°F. Peel turnips and slice off both ends. Spiralize using a small-noodle blade. Place on an aluminum-foil-lined baking sheet and drizzle with 1 tablespoon olive oil and ¼ teaspoon salt. Roast turnips for 10–12 minutes or until they begin to slightly soften.

2 While turnips are roasting, prepare sauce. In a food processor or blender, add cashews, yeast, garlic powder, oregano, rosemary, water, and truffle salt and blend until smooth. Transfer sauce to a small saucepan and heat on medium-low, stirring until sauce thickens. Remove from heat.

3 When noodles are finished roasting, place into a large bowl or pan and pour cream sauce over noodles. Toss until turnip noodles are evenly coated and serve warm.

Kale, Roasted Chickpeas, and Butternut Squash Noodles with Garlic Lemon Tahini Sauce

Isn't it amazing when you can create an entire nutrient-filled dish using just plants? This fiber-filled and colorful side dish is both vegan and gluten-free, slightly inspired by Mediterranean flavors. The wilted, soft kale goes well with the crisp crunch of the chickpeas, and the butternut squash noodles pull this dish together.

Serves 2

1 large butternut squash
2½ tablespoons extra-virgin olive oil, divided
¾ cup canned chickpeas, rinsed and drained
½ teaspoon oregano
½ teaspoon cumin
½ teaspoon garlic powder
2 cups kale

Ingredients for Garlic Lemon Tahini Sauce

2 tablespoons tahini
1 clove garlic, minced
Juice of 1 lemon
1 tablespoon olive oil

1 Preheat oven to 425°F. Cut the bulbous end off your butternut squash and set aside. You will only be using the longer end to spiralize. Peel butternut squash until the top, tough surface is completely removed; then slice in half crosswise and cut off both ends. Spiralize using a small-noodle blade. Place noodles on an aluminum-foil-lined baking sheet and drizzle with 1 tablespoon olive oil. Bake for 10–12 minutes or until noodles are soft. Keep the oven on to roast chickpeas.

2 Place chickpeas in a small bowl and add ½ tablespoon olive oil, oregano, cumin, and garlic powder; toss so chickpeas are evenly coated. Spread on an aluminum-foil-lined baking sheet and bake for about 20–30 minutes or until chickpeas are crispy.

3 While chickpeas are cooking, heat 1 tablespoon olive oil in a large pan on medium heat. Add kale and cook for about 4–5 minutes or until kale is wilted, stirring occasionally and coating the leaves with the oil on the bottom of the pan. When squash and chickpeas are ready, add them to the pan with the kale.

4 Combine tahini, garlic, lemon juice, and olive oil in a small bowl and mix until smooth. Pour over kale mixture and serve warm.

Green Bean and Potato Casserole

Casseroles are American-food favorites, especially around the holidays. This particular casserole is a great addition to Thanksgiving, and what makes it so special is that it's vegan and gluten-free, which means everyone will be able to enjoy the dish despite any dietary restrictions. This dish includes spiralized potato and spiralized onion, meaning you won't spend any extra time chopping or preparing ingredients.

Serves 4-6

1 pound fresh green beans

2 medium onions

4 tablespoons vegetable oil, divided

2 tablespoons whole-wheat flour, divided

1 large russet potato

½ cup raw cashews

1½ cups vegetable broth, divided

½ tablespoon garlic powder

½ tablespoon soy sauce

¼ teaspoon pepper

Fresh Green Beans
Although you can use frozen green beans in this recipe, you're better off using fresh, as it beefs up the casserole and prevents it from getting too mushy or soggy.

1 Preheat oven to 350°F. Bring a pot of water to a boil. Add green beans to pot and cook for 5 minutes. Rinse and drain; set aside.

2 Cut off both ends of the onions and remove the outer layer. Spiralize using a small-noodle blade. Heat 3 tablespoons vegetable oil in a large pan on medium heat. Add onions and cook for 10–11 minutes; let the onions crisp on each side and stir occasionally. About halfway through, add 1 tablespoon flour and mix thoroughly.

3 While onions are cooking, peel the potato. Cut in half crosswise, then slice off both ends. Spiralize using a small-noodle blade. Heat 1 tablespoon vegetable oil in a separate large pan on medium heat. Add potato noodles, cover, and cook for 10 minutes; stir occasionally.

4 Add cashews, 1 cup vegetable broth, garlic powder, soy sauce, and pepper to a blender or food processor and blend until creamy. In a small saucepan or in one of the large pans, heat a small splash of oil on low. Add cashew mixture to slightly heat, stirring constantly. Stir in 1 tablespoon whole-wheat flour until absorbed. Then stir in an additional ¼ cup vegetable broth until absorbed. Return to blender and add another ¼ cup vegetable broth. Blend until smooth.

5 In a large bowl, combine potatoes, green beans, and creamy cashew mixture. Spoon contents into a 7" × 13" baking dish. Top evenly with the fried onions. Bake for 30–45 minutes. Serve warm.

Burmese Noodles

This vegan noodle dish is inspired by the unique cuisine of Myanmar, formerly known as Burma. In these coconut- and spice-flavored noodles, you can see the influence of India and Thailand on Burmese cuisine, from the coconut milk to the curry. Typical ingredients such as ginger, curry, and turmeric are also extremely healthy for the body, known to fight off disease and improve overall health.

Serves 2

- 3 medium zucchini
- 1 tablespoon coconut oil
- 1 tablespoon sesame oil
- 4 cloves garlic, finely minced
- ½ teaspoon grated ginger
- ½ teaspoon turmeric
- ½ teaspoon curry powder
- ¼ teaspoon red chili flakes
- ¼ teaspoon paprika
- ½ cup unsweetened coconut milk
- 1 teaspoon lime juice
- ¼ cup vegetable broth
- 1 tablespoon raw cashews
- 2 stalks green onion
- 1 tablespoon chopped cilantro

1. Peel zucchini, cut in half crosswise, and slice off both ends. Heat coconut oil in a large pan on medium heat and add noodles, tossing so they're coated with the oil. Cook for 4–5 minutes or until noodles begin to soften but are still firm. Set noodles aside.

2. In the same pan, heat sesame oil on medium heat. Add garlic and ginger and cook for 1 minute. Then add turmeric, curry powder, red chili flakes, and paprika, mixing in evenly. Cook for 1 minute.

3. Add coconut milk and lower to a simmer. Stir in lime juice and vegetable broth and simmer for 3 minutes. Add zucchini noodles and mix in until evenly coated with sauce.

4. Use the side of a knife to press down on cashews to crush them. Chop into smaller pieces if desired. Finely chop green onions. Top noodles with crushed cashews, chopped green onions, and cilantro. Serve warm.

Celeriac and Potato Gratin

This creamy side dish uses a combination of celeriac and potatoes, making for a bit more complex flavor than your typical potato gratin. To keep the dish light and less fattening, Greek yogurt is used instead of cream. It's fun to play with texture in this dish; I spiralized the potato and the celeriac with different blades, although you can keep it more standard by using a straight-noodle blade for both, which will give you thin slices that are easily layered.

Serves 4-6

1 large russet potato
1 celeriac root
½ large onion
½ shallot
2 cups Greek yogurt
1½ cups shredded Gruyère cheese, divided
1 clove garlic, minced
1 tablespoon rosemary, divided

1 Preheat oven to 350°F. Grease an 11.5" × 7" baking dish with nonstick cooking spray.

2 Peel potato, cut in half crosswise, and slice off both ends. Spiralize using a small-noodle blade. Place noodles into a large bowl.

3 Cut off rough parts of celeriac root and peel. Make cuts on both ends so you have a smoother surface to spiralize. Spiralize using a straight-noodle blade. Add to the large bowl.

4 Chop onion and shallot and mix in with potato and celeriac. Add mixture to the bottom of the baking sheet.

5 In a medium bowl, mix together Greek yogurt, 1 cup Gruyère, minced garlic, and ½ tablespoon rosemary. Spread over potato and celeriac mixture. Top with ½ cup Gruyère and ½ tablespoon rosemary. Bake for 35 minutes or until top begins to turn golden.

Vegan Zucchini Lasagna

If you're gluten-free or dairy intolerant, you've probably had a moment when you wish you could indulge in something like a nice homemade lasagna. However, just because you can't have wheat or cheese doesn't mean you can't enjoy your own special version, and one that tastes quite similar to the real deal. This vegan and gluten-free lasagna uses zucchini noodles as pasta and blended cashews as ricotta cheese. You'll be amazed at how much the texture resembles a typical lasagna.

Serves 4

- 2 medium zucchini
- ½ large onion
- 2 cloves garlic
- 1 tablespoon extra-virgin olive oil
- 1 (14.5-ounce) can drained diced tomatoes
- 1 cup marinara sauce
- 3 cups spinach
- ½ teaspoon salt, divided
- ¼ teaspoon pepper
- 1 cup raw cashews
- ¼ cup filtered water
- 1 teaspoon garlic powder
- ½ cup chopped fresh basil

1 Preheat oven to 375°F. Cut zucchini in half crosswise and slice off both ends. Spiralize using a straight-noodle blade so noodles come out wavy. Layer half of the spiralized zucchini at the bottom of a 10" × 6" baking pan. Save the other half for a later layer.

2 Chop onions and garlic. In a large pan, heat 1 tablespoon olive oil on medium heat. Add onions and garlic and cook for 4 minutes. Then add diced tomatoes, marinara sauce, spinach, ¼ teaspoon salt, and pepper and cook for 2 minutes. Add half of the sauce as a layer above the zucchini. Save the remaining half for later.

3 Add cashews, filtered water, garlic powder, and ¼ teaspoon salt to a blender or food processor and blend until mixture is almost smooth. There should still be a slightly chunky texture, like that of ricotta cheese. Spread over sauce layer.

4 Cover cashew layer with another layer of zucchini, followed by another layer of sauce. Chop basil and sprinkle over top layer. Cover lasagna with aluminum foil and bake for 30 minutes. Let cool slightly and serve warm.

Kimchi

A traditional Korean side dish made with fermented cabbage, kimchi is a wonderful health food that contains healthy bacteria that helps with digestion. It is also high in vitamins and fiber and low in fat. To make proper kimchi, you should use special Korean red chili flakes, called gochugaru, which give kimchi its distinct flavor. You should be able to find it at an Asian specialty store or online, but if you absolutely can't, you can use regular red chili flakes or other dried peppers. Be warned, though: the taste will not be the same. You can enjoy your kimchi by itself, on a sandwich, in tacos, with eggs, or in rice.

Makes 2 quart-sized jars of Kimchi

1 head napa cabbage
¼ cup sea salt
Filtered water
4 cloves garlic, finely chopped
1 teaspoon grated ginger
3 tablespoons fish sauce
1 tablespoon Korean red chili flakes (gochugaru)
4 stalks green onion
1 large daikon radish (1 cup spiralized)

1 Cut cabbage lengthwise into 4 pieces. Then cut crosswise into 2" pieces. Place cabbage into a large bowl and add salt. Using gloves, massage salt into cabbage until cabbage begins to soften. Add filtered water to the bowl so it covers cabbage. Cover bowl with a lid or a plate and let sit for 2 hours.

2 Rinse cabbage thoroughly under water. Let drain completely in a colander. Squeeze any remaining water out of cabbage.

3 In a small bowl, combine garlic, ginger, fish sauce, and red chili flakes. Mix until it forms a paste.

4 Chop green onion. Peel daikon radish, cut in half crosswise, and slice off both ends. Spiralize using a small-noodle blade, pressing lightly so the noodles come out thinner. Add green onion and radish to bowl with cabbage. Using gloves, mix in paste with cabbage, radish, and green onions. Cabbage should be thoroughly coated.

5 Pack cabbage into a canning jar or Mason jar, leaving a little bit of room at the top. Press down to compress the cabbage, letting the brine rise. Close jar tightly and let sit at room temperature for 1–7 days, then refrigerate. After the first day, open the jar to let the gas release, then reseal. Kimchi is best enjoyed after it has been left out for a week, then refrigerated. Refrigerate for an additional 2 days before eating.

Lentil, Cauliflower, and Radish Bowl

Many people are scared off by the taste of cauliflower, but what they don't realize is that when properly roasted, cauliflower takes on a delicate texture and sweet flavor. Add some lentils for protein and radish for color and crunch, and you have a well-balanced bowl that acts as a perfect side for dinner or when serving guests.

Serves 2–4

- 1 head cauliflower
- 4 tablespoons extra-virgin olive oil, divided
- 1 cup uncooked lentils
- 1 cup water
- 2 Easter egg radishes
- 2 tablespoons white wine vinegar
- Juice of 1 large lemon
- Salt
- Pepper
- Coriander

1 Preheat oven to 400°F. Break off florets of cauliflower from the head and spread on an aluminum-foil-lined baking sheet. Drizzle with 2 tablespoons olive oil and roast for 45 minutes.

2 While cauliflower is cooking, prepare lentils. Add lentils and water to a medium pot and bring to a boil. Once water is boiling, reduce to a simmer, cover, and cook for 30–40 minutes, stirring occasionally. Lentils should be soft but not mushy.

3 Cut ends off of both radishes and spiralize using a straight-noodle blade. The radishes should come out wavy, almost like they were shaved. When cauliflower and lentils are done cooking, toss together with radishes along with 2 tablespoons olive oil, white wine vinegar, lemon juice, and a dash of salt, pepper, and coriander to taste.

Summery Citrus Mint Jicama Noodles

Some people like a little crunch in their noodles, and this light and summery bowl made with jicama is suited for just these people. This refreshing vegan side dish is filled with fresh and airy ingredients, best enjoyed on a hot summer day, though it can be made all year long. Using jicama noodles makes this dish low in calories but high in flavor, and the crunch of the jicama makes a great pairing with the softness of the avocado and grapefruit.

Serves 2

2 large jicamas (2 cups spiralized)

2 tablespoons chopped mint leaves

2 stalks green onion

1 medium grapefruit

½ avocado

¼ cup chopped organic tofu

Juice of 1 lime

2 tablespoons soy sauce

2 tablespoons sesame oil

1 tablespoon hemp seeds

1 Peel jicamas and slice off both ends. Spiralize using a small-noodle blade.

2 Finely chop mint and green onion. Cut grapefruit, avocado, and tofu into small cubes. Toss mint, green onion, grapefruit, avocado, and tofu with jicama noodles.

3 In a small bowl, combine lime juice, soy sauce, and sesame oil. Pour over noodle mixture and toss to coat noodles evenly. Top with hemp seeds and serve at room temperature or chilled.

Why You Should Always Buy Organic Tofu
Tofu can be a wonderful source of protein for vegetarians and vegans, but since it's made with soy, it's important you always buy organic, as nonorganic soy is almost always genetically modified and laden with pesticides.

CHAPTER ELEVEN
Desserts

Homestyle Cinnamon Apple Crumble

This warm and comforting apple dessert is a vegan take on an American classic. Though it doesn't contain any wheat, you can also make the dish gluten-free by making sure to buy oats that haven't been cross-contaminated. The recipe calls for coconut sugar, but you can also use pure maple syrup or brown sugar instead.

Serves 4-6

Ingredients for Filling

4 large Golden Delicious apples

1½ teaspoons cinnamon

2½ tablespoons coconut sugar

2½ teaspoons vanilla

Zest of 1 small lemon

Juice of 1 small lemon

2 tablespoons almond flour

1 tablespoon coconut oil

Ingredients for Crumble

1½ cups almond flour

½ cup old-fashioned oats

5 tablespoons melted coconut oil

3 tablespoons coconut sugar

½ teaspoon salt

1 Preheat oven to 350°F. Spiralize apples using a straight blade, making sure to remove any seeds as you spiralize. Place apples in a large bowl.

2 Add cinnamon, coconut sugar, vanilla, lemon zest, lemon juice, and almond flour and mix until apples are evenly coated.

3 Grease a 7" × 13" baking dish with 1 tablespoon coconut oil. Spread apple mixture evenly across pan.

4 To prepare crumble topping, combine almond flour, oats, coconut oil, coconut sugar, and salt and mix until mixture forms little balls. Spoon evenly over apple mixture.

5 Bake for about 20–25 minutes until crumble is crispy and apples are soft and bubbling. Let cool for about 15 minutes and then serve warm.

Zucchini Chocolate Soufflé

This dairy-free, flourless chocolate soufflé tastes fluffy and decadent, but it has a little secret ingredient: zucchini. This is a great way to sneak in a vegetable while enjoying a sweet treat. This soufflé is also gluten-free and dairy-free, making it a great choice for people with sensitive stomachs. It's also quick to prepare, and you can even make an individual portion if you ever feel like treating yourself.

Makes 4 soufflés

½ tablespoon coconut oil

5 tablespoons unsweetened almond milk, divided

4 tablespoons maple syrup

4 tablespoons cocoa powder

2 large cage-free egg yolks

1 medium zucchini

4 cage-free egg whites

2 tablespoons coconut sugar

Ingredients for Chocolate Sauce

4 tablespoons coconut oil

2 tablespoons maple syrup

4 tablespoons cocoa powder

1 Preheat oven to 375°F. Grease 4 small ramekins with coconut oil.

2 In a small saucepan, heat 3 tablespoons almond milk until just below a boil. Add maple syrup and cocoa powder and stir for 1–2 minutes or until mixture gets smooth. Add egg yolks and stir in for 1–2 minutes. Remove from heat.

3 Cut zucchini in half crosswise and slice off both ends. Spiralize using a small-noodle blade. If your noodles come out long, break them up into smaller pieces so they can be separated into the soufflés.

4 Return saucepan to low heat and add zucchini to saucepan along with remaining 2 tablespoons almond milk. Stir until zucchini is evenly coated. Remove from heat.

5 In a medium bowl, add egg whites and coconut sugar. Whip until frothy. Fold ½ of egg white mixture into chocolate mixture. Then fold the batter into the rest of the egg whites. Transfer batter to ramekins, filling about ½–¾ full.

6 Place in the oven and bake for 25–30 minutes. In a small bowl, combine 4 tablespoons coconut oil with 2 tablespoons maple syrup and 4 tablespoons cocoa powder. Transfer to a saucepan to warm on low heat for 1 minute. Pour over soufflés and serve warm.

Almond Cake with Pumpkin-Spiced Butternut Squash

Squash is often prepared in savory dishes, but the winter vegetable is naturally sweet in flavor and, like pumpkin, can be used in desserts. In fact, squash can be flavored in the same way as pumpkin, as this recipe uses a premade pumpkin pie spice mixture commonly found in grocery stores. This almond cake isn't super sweet, but if you prefer it sweeter, you can increase the amount of maple syrup you add or top the cake with powdered sugar once it's done baking.

Serves 4–6

- ½ cup almond flour
- 2 large cage-free eggs
- 1 egg white
- ¼ cup unsweetened almond milk
- 2 tablespoons pure maple syrup
- 3 tablespoons melted coconut oil, divided
- ¼ cup sliced raw almonds
- 1 medium butternut squash
- 1 teaspoon coconut oil
- 1 tablespoon pumpkin pie spice
- Optional: coconut sugar or powdered sugar

1 Preheat oven to 350°F. In a large bowl, mix almond flour, eggs, egg white, almond milk, maple syrup, and 2 tablespoons melted coconut oil. Whip until mix is frothy.

2 Pour 1 tablespoon melted coconut oil onto the bottom of a cast-iron skillet and swirl around until coated. Pour cake mixture into skillet. Sprinkle almond slices onto batter. Place in the oven and cook for 25–30 minutes or until cake is firm and golden.

3 While cake is cooking, spiralize squash. Slice off bulb and peel remaining squash, removing all outer skin. Using a straight-noodle blade, spiralize squash so it comes out in big, round pieces, enough to fill about ¾ cup.

4 In a small pan, heat 1 teaspoon coconut oil on medium heat. Add squash to pan and top with pumpkin pie spice mixture. Cover and cook for about 7 minutes until squash is soft.

5 Remove cake from the oven and top with squash. Sprinkle with coconut sugar or powdered sugar if desired. Let cool for about 15–20 minutes. Cake can be served warm or at room temperature.

Pumpkin Zucchini Muffins with Cherries

Pumpkin and zucchini are both fall staples, and they both happen to taste great in baked goods, so why not put them together? If you've ever had zucchini bread, you know how well zucchini cooks into pastries, making them moist and tender. Although the zucchini is spiralized, it bakes nicely into these muffins, and you might not even notice its presence (though you will notice how moist and delicious these muffins are!). You may even be tempted to whip this dessert out at Thanksgiving dinner.

Makes 1 dozen muffins

Cupcake liners
Nonstick baking spray
2 medium zucchini (1 cup spiralized)
1 cup pumpkin purée
½ cup almond milk
¼ cup coconut oil
½ cup dried cherries
½ cup almond flour
½ cup whole-wheat flour
½ cup coconut sugar
2 teaspoons pumpkin pie spice
½ teaspoon salt
2 teaspoons baking powder

1 Preheat oven to 375°F. Place cupcake liners in a muffin tin and spray bottom and sides with cooking spray. Set aside.

2 Peel zucchini, cut in half crosswise, and slice off both ends. Spiralize using a small-noodle blade. Break up noodle pieces using a knife so that they are no larger than 2″ thick. You should have about 1 cup of zucchini noodles.

3 In a large bowl, whisk together pumpkin purée, almond milk, and coconut oil until well combined. Then mix in zucchini and dried cherries.

4 In a separate large bowl, combine almond flour, whole-wheat flour, coconut sugar, pumpkin pie spice, salt, and baking powder. Mix until well combined.

5 Gradually pour the wet ingredients into the dry ingredients. Rather than stirring everything together, gradually fold wet into dry using a wooden spoon, continuing to lightly fold both mixtures together until evenly combined.

6 Evenly distribute batter into muffin tins, filling cups almost to the top and leaving about ½″ of space. Bake for 25–30 minutes or until tops of muffins are firm. Let cool and serve.

Spiralized Fruit Salad with Coconut Whipped Cream

For those of us who like to consume sugar the natural way, fruit is our go-to for dessert. Spiralizing apples and pears for this fruit salad makes this dish a little more exciting, and it almost feels like you're eating your own bowl of dessert noodles. Fruit salad doesn't feel complete without a side of whipped cream, but you wouldn't want to sabotage your healthy eating habits with an addition of heavy cream and sugar. Instead, you can make this dairy-free, two-ingredient coconut whipped cream, which just uses coconut milk and coconut sugar.

Serves 4

1 apple
1 pear
1 cup red grapes
1 cup blueberries
1 cup chopped strawberries
½ lemon

Ingredients for Coconut Whipped Cream

1 cup coconut milk
½ tablespoon coconut sugar

1 Remove stem from apple and pear. Spiralize both using a small-noodle blade. Using a knife, slightly break up noodles, then place noodles in a large bowl and toss them together.

2 In a medium bowl, combine grapes, blueberries, and strawberries, mixing together. Pour mixed fruits on top of apple and pear noodles. Squeeze lemon over fruit salad mixture. This will help keep fruit from going brown when exposed to the air.

3 To make coconut whipped cream, add coconut milk and coconut sugar to a blender and whip until coconut forms soft peaks. Serve on top of fruit or with a spoon on the side.

Cinnamon-Sugar Sweet Potato Fries

My guilty-pleasure food has always been French fries. When I'm having an ultimate junk-food craving, I always want fries, so it would make sense that I would try to find a healthy way to enjoy them at any time of the day. These sweet potato fries are coated in coconut oil and seasoned with coconut sugar and cinnamon to make them a sweet treat. If you don't have coconut sugar, regular sugar can be used as well. The advantage to coconut sugar is that it is lower in fructose than regular refined cane sugar.

Serves 2–4

2 large sweet potatoes
2 tablespoons melted
   coconut oil
¼ cup coconut sugar
¾ teaspoon cinnamon

1 Preheat oven to 425°F. Cut sweet potatoes in half crosswise and cut off both ends. Spiralize using a large-noodle blade. Place into a large bowl and toss with coconut oil.

2 Spread sweet potatoes evenly on an aluminum-foil-lined baking sheet. In a small bowl, combine coconut sugar and cinnamon. Sprinkle half the mixture over the sweet potatoes. Bake for 10 minutes and then flip fries over. Cook for an additional 15–20 minutes until sweet potatoes begin to crisp.

3 Remove from oven and sprinkle with remaining cinnamon sugar. Let cool for 5 minutes and serve warm.

Plantain Rice Pudding

When plantains are ripe, they take on a much sweeter flavor, making them a great substitute in rice pudding. Though you still need to get a fairly green plantain to be able to spiralize it, it's okay if it is beginning to ripen a little bit, as it will only enhance the caramel-like flavor. If you prefer your pudding extra sweet, add more maple syrup to the recipe, or drizzle some over the finished product. You can also serve the pudding with fruit, raisins, nuts, or any toppings you may desire.

Serves 2

1 large plantain
1 tablespoon coconut oil
½ cup coconut milk, divided
2–3 tablespoons maple syrup
2 teaspoons vanilla
2 teaspoons cinnamon

1 Remove peel from plantain, cut in half cross-wise, and slice off both ends. Spiralize using a small-noodle blade.

2 In a medium pan, heat 1 tablespoon coconut oil on medium heat. Add plantain noodles and sauté for about 1 minute. Then, as plantains begin to cook and soften, break them up into little rice-sized pieces using a spatula. This should naturally occur as plantains begin cooking. Sauté for about 2–3 minutes and then remove from heat.

3 While plantains are cooking, heat ¼ cup coconut milk in a saucepan until it just hits a boil. Lower to medium heat and add plantain rice, maple syrup, vanilla, and cinnamon and mix together. Cook for about 3–5 minutes until coconut milk is absorbed, stirring occasionally. Then add the remaining ¼ cup coconut milk and stir until coconut milk is absorbed again. Serve warm or let rice cool and then refrigerate.

No-Churn Coconut Ice Cream with Apples and Caramel

If you've ever had a slice of apple pie à la mode, you know how delicious the combination of warm apples and ice cream is. It's a classic American dessert but one that is also filled with a lot of sugar and dairy. This version of caramel apple ice cream is dairy-free and refined-sugar-free, making it a great choice if you're trying to please people with various dietary restrictions. The best part is you don't need an ice cream maker to whip up this creamy frozen treat. All you need is a freezer and one night of patience.

Serves 4

Ingredients for Ice Cream
- ½ cup dates
- ¼ cup filtered water
- 1 teaspoon vanilla
- 2 cups full-fat unsweetened coconut milk

Ingredients for Apples
- 2 apples
- 1 tablespoon coconut oil
- ¼ teaspoon cinnamon

Ingredients for Caramel Sauce
- ½ cup dates
- 2 tablespoons unsweetened almond milk
- 1 tablespoon pure maple syrup

Serving Ice Cream

The coconut ice cream will be extremely frozen when removed from the freezer. It's important to let it soften for about 10 minutes (or possibly longer) to be able to serve. Use an ice cream scooper to create nice-looking scoops, and don't leave it out too long or it will begin to melt and lose its consistency.

1 Soak dates in warm water for 10 minutes and then drain. Combine dates with filtered water in a blender or food processor and blend until it forms a smooth paste. Set aside.

2 Combine vanilla and coconut milk in a blender and blend until coconut milk is frothy. Add date paste and blend until smooth.

3 Line a freezer-safe container with parchment paper and pour coconut milk mixture into container. Cover with plastic wrap and then aluminum foil and then freeze overnight.

4 When you are ready to eat ice cream, prepare apples. Spiralize apples using a small-noodle blade. Then heat 1 tablespoon coconut oil in a medium pan on medium heat. Add apples and cinnamon and sauté for 1–2 minutes until apples just begin to soften. Place into bottom of bowls.

5 Remove ice cream from freezer and let sit for about 10 minutes to allow ice cream to soften. Prepare caramel sauce by adding dates, almond milk, and maple syrup to a blender or food processor and blend until smooth. Then add to a small saucepan and cook on medium for about 2 minutes or until warm.

6 Scoop ice cream from container and add on top of apples. Top with caramel sauce and enjoy immediately.

Apple Bread Pudding

Bread pudding is an international dish, but in the United States especially it's prepared and served as a dessert. Adding in spiralized apples helps give the bread pudding more flavor and keeps it moist, and since it's easily made in large quantities, it's a great option when entertaining. Challah bread is used here because it has a sweeter flavor, but you don't have to limit yourself to that particular kind of bread. If you want to be healthier, you can opt for something baked with whole wheat, or you can use any day-old bread you have on hand.

Serves 6

Nonstick cooking spray or
  coconut oil
1 challah bread loaf
4 medium apples (2 cups
  spiralized)
2 cups unsweetened almond
  milk
½ cup coconut sugar
4 cage-free eggs
1 teaspoon cinnamon
1 teaspoon vanilla
¼ teaspoon salt

1 Preheat oven to 350°F. Spray an 11.5" × 7" baking dish with nonstick spray or rub with coconut oil. Break bread into small pieces and create a bottom layer in your baking dish. Remove stems from the apples and cut off both ends. Spiralize with a small-noodle blade. Top bread layer with spiralized apples.

2 In a medium bowl, combine almond milk, coconut sugar, eggs, cinnamon, vanilla, and salt. Mix until smooth. Pour batter over bread and apples. Bake for 30–40 minutes and serve warm.

Berry Smoothie Bowl with Pear

My favorite desserts tend to be the most natural, which make fruit-heavy options my favorite. Smoothie bowls are a good choice because they remind me of ice cream, and you can also fill them up with toppings, which you can't do when they're in a glass. All you need are frozen bananas and your choice of accompanying fruit, as well as any other nuts and seeds to top it off, and you've got yourself a healthy rival to ice cream or frozen yogurt.

Serves 2

Ingredients for Smoothie

3 frozen bananas

½ cup raspberries

½ cup strawberries

⅓ cup unsweetened almond milk

Ingredients for Toppings

1 pear

7 or 8 raspberries

1 tablespoon chia seeds

1 tablespoon pomegranate seeds

5 or 6 blackberries

1. Combine frozen bananas, raspberries, strawberries, and almond milk in a blender and blend together until smooth. Pour into a bowl.

2. To spiralize pear, remove stem, cut off both ends, and spiralize using a small-noodle blade. Place in the corner of your bowl. Add topping ingredients in a diagonal line, starting with raspberries and ending with blackberries. Serve immediately.

Breakfast Bowl

If you want to turn your smoothie bowl into a breakfast bowl, consider adding some greens or nuts to give you a morning boost of nutrition.

Plantain Mango Sticky Rice

Sticky rice with mango is an essential Thai treat. Like rice pudding, it is flavored with coconut, a Thai staple, but it is often served in a ball or solid form rather than a pudding, and it is dressed with a gooey, sweet coconut sauce. I use coconut sugar in this recipe, but it does darken the color of both the plantains and the coconut sauce. If you prefer to keep your rice light and your sauce white, as it traditionally looks, you can use regular white sugar instead.

Serves 4

2 large plantains
½ tablespoon coconut oil
1½ cups coconut milk
2 tablespoons coconut sugar
1 medium mango

Ingredients for Coconut Sauce

1 cup unsweetened coconut milk
2 tablespoons coconut sugar

Not Mango Season?
If mango is not in season, you can also make this dessert with coconut or banana, other Thai dessert staples. Or, experiment with other fruits you love.

1 Peel plantains, cut in half crosswise, and slice off both ends of the plantains. Spiralize using a small-noodle blade.

2 Heat coconut oil in a medium pan on medium heat. Add plantains and stir around in coconut oil, cooking for about 1 minute. As plantains cook, break them into rice-sized pieces with a spatula. This should naturally happen as the plantain softens. Cook for about 3 minutes, stirring frequently so bottoms of plantains don't burn.

3 While plantains are cooking, bring 1 cup coconut milk to a boil. Return to medium heat and add coconut sugar and plantain rice. Cook for 3–4 minutes, stirring frequently until coconut milk is absorbed. Add remaining ½ cup coconut milk and stir for 1–2 minutes until the coconut milk is almost fully absorbed but the rice is still moist and sticky.

4 Prepare mango by peeling from top to bottom. Stand the mango up and look where the mango is the widest (known as the cheeks of the mango). Slice both cheeks off the mango, then cut into 1″ wedges. Slice the remaining fruit off of the pit, then slice into smaller, 1″ wedges.

5 To make coconut sauce, bring 1 cup coconut milk to almost a boil, then lower to medium-low heat. Add coconut sugar and stir in, mixing evenly.

6 Serve sticky rice with mango on the side and drizzle coconut sauce over rice. Serve warm.

Mini Pear Tarts

Making pastries may seem daunting, but these tarts are easy enough even for the novice home chef. Basic baking ingredients and a muffin tin are all that you need to make your own tarts from scratch at home. These tarts are made healthier using a blend of oat flour, whole-wheat flour, and almond flour for the crust, and just a little bit of natural sweetener in the filling. If you don't happen to have any pears on hand, apples can work for this recipe as well.

Makes 6 tarts

Ingredients for Tart Dough

- ¼ cup oat flour (can blend old-fashioned oats to make flour as well)
- ½ cup whole-wheat flour
- ½ cup almond flour
- 1 cage-free egg yolk
- 2 tablespoons melted coconut oil
- 2 tablespoons melted ghee (clarified butter)
- ½ teaspoon salt

Ingredients for Filling

- 1 large Bartlett pear
- 2 tablespoons coconut sugar
- 2 tablespoons pure maple syrup
- 1 teaspoon lemon juice
- ½ teaspoon vanilla

1 Preheat oven to 350°F. In a medium bowl, combine oat flour, whole-wheat flour, and almond flour. Mix in egg yolk, melted coconut oil, melted ghee, and salt. Transfer to a blender and blend until smooth. The dough should be pretty thick and chunky.

2 Transfer dough to the bottom of a muffin tin, making 6 muffins. Press the bottoms flat and form the sides so they go halfway up the tin. Bake for 5 minutes and remove from oven.

3 Slice off both ends of pear and spiralize using a small-noodle blade. Use a knife to slightly break up noodles. Combine pear noodles with coconut sugar, maple syrup, lemon juice, and vanilla. Fill each dough-packed muffin tin with pear mixture. Bake for 30 minutes or until top begins to become golden and tart becomes slightly crisp. Let cool and serve.

Apple Granola Bars

Granola bars have long been touted as a health food, but if you're going for the store-bought ones, you're not exactly eating something nutritious. Many common granola bars are processed and filled with refined carbohydrates and added sugars, but you can quickly make your own at home using natural ingredients and real apples. These bars can be enjoyed instantly warm, or they can be cut up and taken as a snack throughout the week.

Makes 8 bars

½ teaspoon coconut oil
1 cup old-fashioned oats
¼ cup almond flour
¼ cup coconut sugar
¼ cup almond slivers
¼ teaspoon cardamom
¼ teaspoon nutmeg
½ teaspoon cinnamon
½ teaspoon vanilla
1–2 medium apples (1 cup
  spiralized)

1 Preheat oven to 350°F. Grease an 8″ × 8″ baking pan with coconut oil.

2 In a large bowl, combine oats, flour, coconut sugar, almonds, cardamom, nutmeg, cinnamon, and vanilla.

3 Remove stems from apples, cut off both ends, and spiralize with a small-noodle blade; break noodles up using a knife. Mix in with the rest of the ingredients. Spoon mixture into the baking pan and press flat with a spoon. Bake for 10–15 minutes or until granola is golden. Let cool and slice into quarters vertically. Then cut in half lengthwise.

Red Velvet Beet Chocolate Chip Cookies

The red velvet flavor has grown in popularity over the last few years, and with its subtle chocolate flavor, it's hard not to understand why. Unfortunately, many red velvet baked goods are dyed with red food coloring, which isn't so great for our health. In these cookies, there's no need to use red dyes; the natural color of the beets gives these cookies a red tinge. Since beets are naturally sweet, they also add flavor to the cookies, making them a tasty as well as attractive dessert option.

Makes 1 dozen cookies

3 large red beets
½ cup coconut sugar
¼ cup pure maple syrup
¼ cup melted coconut oil
½ teaspoon apple cider vinegar
1 cup whole-wheat flour
1 cup almond flour
½ tablespoon baking powder
½ cup chocolate chips

1 Preheat oven to 350°F. Peel beets and slice off both ends. Spiralize using a small-noodle blade. Take half of the beets and put them into a blender; purée until smooth. Keep the other half spiralized and use a knife to break up the noodles into smaller pieces.

2 In a large bowl, combine spiralized beets, puréed beets, coconut sugar, maple syrup, coconut oil, and apple cider vinegar until mixed evenly. In a separate medium bowl, combine whole-wheat flour, almond flour, baking powder, and chocolate chips.

3 Mix dry ingredients into wet ingredients until smooth. Grease a baking sheet with a little bit of coconut oil. Spoon 12 mounds of batter onto baking sheet, pressing down to flatten slightly into a cookie shape. Bake for 10–15 minutes. Let cool for about 10 minutes and then serve.

Sweet Potato Pecan Pie

If you're looking to spiralize around the holidays, this dessert is for you. A swirly take on a classic sweet potato pecan pie, this version is all-natural and looks extra special when cut open. The recipe calls for a premade crust, but if you're feeling adventurous, you can also make one on your own. This pie is filled with sweetness and spice, making it a good option for Thanksgiving or Christmas.

Serves 6

2 large sweet potatoes
2 tablespoons coconut oil
½ cup almond milk
½ cup coconut sugar
1 teaspoon vanilla
¼ teaspoon allspice
1 teaspoon cinnamon
¼ teaspoon nutmeg
¼ teaspoon ground cloves
1 unbaked crust of choice
    (I prefer whole-wheat or
    gluten-free crusts)

Ingredients for Pecan Topping

1 large cage-free egg
¼ cup coconut sugar
¼ cup pure maple syrup
1 tablespoon melted ghee
    (clarified butter)
½ cup pecans

1 Preheat oven to 350°F. Peel sweet potatoes, cut in half crosswise, and slice off both ends. Spiralize using a small-noodle blade. In a large pan, heat 2 tablespoons coconut oil on medium heat. Add sweet potatoes, cover, and cook for about 7–10 minutes or until sweet potatoes are very soft.

2 Combine potatoes with almond milk, coconut sugar, vanilla, allspice, cinnamon, nutmeg, and cloves. Scoop mixture into the pie crust, slightly flattening the top.

3 In a small bowl, whisk 1 egg with coconut sugar. Then add maple syrup and melted ghee and combine until smooth. Then add pecans and mix until they are coated evenly.

4 Top sweet potato mixture with pecans. Bake for about 45 minutes until filling is set and pecans begin to slightly brown. Let cool and refrigerate for at least 1 hour before serving.

Strawberry and Apple Chia Seed Pudding

Adding little fiber-filled chia seeds to foods can help you get an extra dose of nutrients, as well as keep you full and hydrated throughout the day. These seeds may look normal when you first see them, but once they're submerged in liquid, they expand and take on a gummy-like texture. Make a big batch of them, and they turn something like almond milk into a tasty pudding. Don't believe me? Try it for yourself. Make sure to let your mixture sit overnight to get the right texture, and if your pudding isn't thick enough by morning, you can always mix in another ¼ cup of chia seeds.

Serves 2–4

- 2 cups unsweetened almond milk
- ½ cup chia seeds
- 2 tablespoons pure maple syrup
- ½ teaspoon vanilla
- 1 medium apple
- 2 cups strawberries

1. In a large bowl, combine almond milk, chia seeds, maple syrup, and vanilla. Stir until chia seeds are mixed in evenly. Cover and let sit for 30 minutes. If any chia seeds have settled or become chunky, mix again until even. Cover and refrigerate overnight.

2. In the morning, check to see if pudding has thickened. If it has, spoon mixture into a stemless wine glass, Mason jar, or cup; leave a 1" space at the top.

3. Remove stem, cut off both ends, and spiralize apple with a small-noodle blade; top pudding with apples. Slice strawberries and add to the top. Serve cool.

Trying Different Flavors
Chia seed pudding doesn't have to be just vanilla flavored. Trying mixing in other flavors such as pumpkin purée or cocoa powder to experiment with different kinds of pudding. Just mix in before refrigerating.

Carrot Cake with Cream Cheese Frosting

I've never been a huge fan of carrot cake—that is, until I made my own. Most store-bought versions I've tried have been dry and tasteless, but not this one. This spiralized carrot cake is moist, full of spices, and just the right amount of sweet. By spiralizing your carrots, and then slightly blending them, you save a bunch of time, as you don't have to labor over grating your carrots. The spiralized carrots also provide a fun, and healthy, topping for the cake. You can experiment with how to incorporate the spiralized carrots into the design of your carrot cake, but at least you know your dessert will not only be pretty but filled with healthy and clean ingredients.

Yields 1 cake (serves 8–10)

- 5 jumbo carrots (5 cups spiralized)
- 3 cups coconut sugar
- 1 cup coconut oil
- ½ cup vegetable oil
- 8 large cage-free eggs
- ⅔ cup Greek yogurt
- 4 tablespoons pure maple syrup
- 2 teaspoons vanilla
- 5 cups whole-wheat flour
- 1½ teaspoons baking powder
- 1 teaspoon cinnamon plus a couple dashes, divided
- 1 teaspoon ground cloves
- ½ tablespoon melted coconut oil
- 1 (16-ounce) tub cream cheese (can be full-fat or low-fat)
- 2 teaspoons vanilla
- ½ cup powdered sugar
- 1 tablespoon pure maple syrup
- ¼ cup pecan halves

1 Preheat oven to 350°F. Grease and flour two (9") cake pans. Cut carrots in half and slice off both ends. Spiralize using a small-noodle blade. Set aside.

2 In a large bowl, combine coconut sugar, coconut oil, vegetable oil, eggs, Greek yogurt, maple syrup, and vanilla until smooth.

3 In a separate medium bowl, combine whole-wheat flour, baking powder, 1 teaspoon cinnamon, and cloves. Gradually pour these dry ingredients into the wet ingredients, mixing in thoroughly.

4 Place 4 cups of the spiralized carrots (leave the remaining 1 cup for the top of the cake) into a blender and lightly pulse so carrots become shredded (but not puréed). Mix carrots thoroughly into cake batter.

5 Divide batter evenly into the 2 cake pans and place in the oven. Bake for 25–35 minutes or until top begins to get slightly golden. You can check if cake is ready by inserting a toothpick into the middle: The toothpick should come out clean. If there is batter on it, it needs to be cooked for longer.

6 When cakes are ready, remove from oven and place on a wire rack to cool. Turn oven temperature to 425°F. Put remaining carrot noodles on an aluminum-foil-lined baking sheet and lightly drizzle with melted coconut oil. Top with a dash of cinnamon if desired. Bake for 10 minutes or until carrots begin to soften.

7 Prepare frosting by mixing together cream cheese, vanilla, powdered sugar, and maple syrup by hand or with a mixer. Once cakes have cooled, spread frosting on the top of one cake. Place the other cake on top of it. If your cakes are bumpy or uneven, you may need to cut the top off of each to even out the surface. Once the top cake is on the bottom cake, ice the rest of the cake, including the top and all sides.

8 Top with roasted spiralized carrots and pecans. If you want to get fancy, you can place the noodles so they create a swirl on the top, and the pecans can be placed around the perimeter of the cake to create a border. Top with a dash of cinnamon if desired.

Metric Conversion Chart

VOLUME CONVERSIONS

U.S. Volume Measure	Metric Equivalent
⅛ teaspoon	0.5 milliliter
¼ teaspoon	1 milliliter
½ teaspoon	2 milliliters
1 teaspoon	5 milliliters
½ tablespoon	7 milliliters
1 tablespoon (3 teaspoons)	15 milliliters
2 tablespoons (1 fluid ounce)	30 milliliters
¼ cup (4 tablespoons)	60 milliliters
⅓ cup	90 milliliters
½ cup (4 fluid ounces)	125 milliliters
⅔ cup	160 milliliters
¾ cup (6 fluid ounces)	180 milliliters
1 cup (16 tablespoons)	250 milliliters
1 pint (2 cups)	500 milliliters
1 quart (4 cups)	1 liter (about)

WEIGHT CONVERSIONS

U.S. Weight Measure	Metric Equivalent
½ ounce	15 grams
1 ounce	30 grams
2 ounces	60 grams
3 ounces	85 grams
¼ pound (4 ounces)	115 grams
½ pound (8 ounces)	225 grams
¾ pound (12 ounces)	340 grams
1 pound (16 ounces)	454 grams

OVEN TEMPERATURE CONVERSIONS

Degrees Fahrenheit	Degrees Celsius
200 degrees F	95 degrees C
250 degrees F	120 degrees C
275 degrees F	135 degrees C
300 degrees F	150 degrees C
325 degrees F	160 degrees C
350 degrees F	180 degrees C
375 degrees F	190 degrees C
400 degrees F	205 degrees C
425 degrees F	220 degrees C
450 degrees F	230 degrees C

BAKING PAN SIZES

American	Metric
8 x 1½ inch round baking pan	20 x 4 cm cake tin
9 x 1½ inch round baking pan	23 x 3.5 cm cake tin
11 x 7 x 1½ inch baking pan	28 x 18 x 4 cm baking tin
13 x 9 x 2 inch baking pan	30 x 20 x 5 cm baking tin
2 quart rectangular baking dish	30 x 20 x 3 cm baking tin
15 x 10 x 2 inch baking pan	30 x 25 x 2 cm baking tin (Swiss roll tin)
9 inch pie plate	22 x 4 or 23 x 4 cm pie plate
7 or 8 inch springform pan	18 or 20 cm springform or loose bottom cake tin
9 x 5 x 3 inch loaf pan	23 x 13 x 7 cm or 2 lb narrow loaf or pate tin
1½ quart casserole	1.5 liter casserole
2 quart casserole	2 liter casserole

Index

About the Author

Carina Wolff is a health and wellness journalist located in Santa Monica, California. She covers food, nutrition, and wellness for a variety of websites, and runs her own health food blog, *Kale Me Maybe*, where she creates healthy plant-based, clean-eating recipes. Her philosophy on food is that it should be healthy and accessible, but still tasty enough that you can enjoy what you eat. You can find her blog at *www.kalememaybe.com*.